MY FORTUNE

V.S. GURUSWAMY

"SRI GAYATRI"
No. 14, Srinivasan Street,
Mandaveli, Chennai – 600 028.
Tamil Nadu, India.
Email: myfortune6@gmail.com
Web Address: www.myfortune.org

ALL ABOUT THIS BOOK

Publisher : GURUSWAMY LLC

ISBN 978-8 1-928275-2- 0

© V.S. Guruswamy
"Sri Gayatri"
No. 14, Srinivasan Street,
Mandaveli, Chennai – 600 028.
Tamil Nadu, India.
Email: myfortune6@gmail.com

Web Address: www.myfortune.org

V.S. GURUSWAMY, M.A.

 # CONTENTS

CHALDEAN SYSTEM OF NUMEROLOGY

LETTER	NUMBER	RULER
A,I,J,Q,Y	1	SUN
B,K,R	2	MOON
C,G,L,S	3	JUPITER
D, M, T	4	URANUS
E,H,N,X	5	MERCURY
U,V,W	6	VENUS
O, Z	7	NEPTUNE
F,P	8	SATURN
--	9	MARS

(The table given above is based on the CHALDEAN system, a rather ancient but accurate system. Because of its "Mystic" nature dealing with the invisible forces at work in human lives, the interpretations are simplified in this book)

INTRODUCTION

"The GURU of Fortune"

Mr. V.S. Guruswamy, the youngest son of Pandit Sethuraman, was born in the year of 1963 at Madras. He is the author of this book, "My Fortune".

Pandit Sethuraman was, by then, at the peak of his fame as a Numerologist both at home and abroad. This Messiah of Numerology, despite his busy routine of giving occult guidance to hundreds of his clients every day, ensured proper initiation of his son, Guruswamy into the art of predicting one's life through numbers and names.

Guruswamy, when he turned fifteen, started learning the science of the mystic numbers under the strict surveillance of his illustrious father and Guru. He travelled widely to many parts of the world and endeared himself to his clients. Guruswamy did not neglect the academic studies. He passed his M.A. having studied at Vivekananda College, Madras, India.

Reading, writing and continuous research are Mr. Guruswamy's forte! Happily married and having become father of two children, this responsible husband and affectionate father continues his profession as the leading Numerologist, undeterred by the burden of swelling number of clients and his frequent tours abroad. The tragedy of having lost his father and mentor Pandit Sethuraman in the year 1997, has not impeded his spirit. On the other hand, he took efforts in publishing the fourteenth edition of "Adhishta Vingyanam" (Tamil), the classic treatise on the subject of Numerology and magnum opus of his father who first published it in 1954. What more, Guruswamy translated it and published the first English edition of the book, entitled "Science of Fortune" in 2003 which has become the all-time best seller in India and abroad. To cap it all, he had this book published in five languages including Chinese, which feat no Indian author of occultism has ever performed so far!

MY FORTUNE

Times changed, so did the fortunes of people! As the mantle of profession fell on the shoulders of Guruswamy, he took up the great responsibility of catering to the needs of multitudes of his clients, both old and the new. His became a rigorous routine because of the swelling clientele and lack of time. But his research on the subject of Numerology continued. Now, his findings about the "Destiny" numbers revealed a new world to him. This must be shared with those who are frantically searching for money, success and spouse. Thus was born the book namely, **"My Fortune"**. It is not just a sequel to his illustrious father's work, but a compendium of comprehensive predictions which present a compelling reader. Frantically searching for success in our professional and personal lives, we must consider ourselves fortunate in our quest, if we have this book, "My Fortune" which is the best!

This book needs no introduction, since every line of its contents introduces the author Mr.Guruswamy and his original ideas based on years of his research and experience. His calibre and ability to improve the fortunes of ill-managed corporates or individuals has won world wide acclaim. His numerological advice had added succour to the lives of suffering masses and also helped ailing families achieve harmony and peace. Though success or happiness is achieved by sailing hard in the sea of troubles in bad weather, "My Fortune" of Mr. Guruswamy will certainly make your journey easy, smooth, and profitable. I am sure that this valuable book serves you as a guide and companion throughout your life!

Affable, humorous, intelligent and industrious, Mr. Guruswamy, as claimed by his clientele, has filled the vacuum caused by the demise of his father and mentor, Pandit Sethuraman. But, this young and successful Numerologist of international fame, modestly denies this claim! "Panditji is incomparable!", he says!!.

S.Gopinath

FOREWORD

It is with immense pleasure that I present this work of mine, "My Fortune" not only to those who believe in the magic of numbers that shape their destiny, but also to the fair-minded skeptics. This is basically a compendium of secrets about the dates on which you were born, the current of your destiny and to what extent you can progress in your life. My long years of research, experience and also the blessings of my father and mentor, Pandit Sethuraman, have helped me in bringing out this book, in the best possible manner. "My Fortune" is all-inclusive and reader friendly. It gives lucid interpretations about your Birth, Destiny and Name numbers which will be fascinating and also meaningful. The synchronicities that would emerge after your reading this book may be astoundingly similar to the events in your life. I am sure that the readers find this book their lifetime companion!

Friends! The noble principle of human life is to "live and let live". It is possible only when you proceed in the right direction with the right purpose. I have given you a perfect vehicle for finding your fortune and you have commenced your journey.

I wish you a happy and memorable journey!

V.S. Guruswamy

NUMEROLOGY -
THE MYSTIC KEY TO SUCCESS

Numbers and names are inseparably connected to human life. They are the foundation of evolution without which the human race could not have progressed to the present state. How many of us know that salamanders always choose their meal of insects only on the basis of their numbers; Rhesus monkeys select only those trees for plucking fruits whichever having greater number of fruits and a particular breed of shepherd dogs in the southern America "count" the number of cattle before returning home by hopping over each of them? Man, the noblest creation of God, depends immensely on numbers in every activity of his life. He knows that a world devoid of numbers and names would end up in chaos and cease to exist subsequently. Educational institutions, elections, financial institutions like banks, lotteries, telephones, computers, airlines and even prisons employ the use of NUMBERS which are indispensable to man and his routine transactions. He may claim that he has conquered Nature and invented the modern sciences with the power of his intellect. But, he is yet to decipher the remaining ninety nine percent of the "Divine code of God". Animals act as per their instincts, but the rational animal called "Man" acts as and how his "Wisdom" suggests. It was this wisdom of man that gifted him a wonderful science of "peeping into future", called NUMEROLOGY - knowing all aspects of one's life through numbers!

MY FORTUNE

Numerology, one of the earliest predictive sciences the human race knows and practices, is actually dealing with the planets in the solar family and the cosmological forces they emit. These forces that affect the plant and animal life on the earth vary in their strength depending upon the planet from which they emanate. Thus, when the necessity for identifying such cosmological forces and their results arose, the planets were represented by NUMBERS and NAMES revealing their occult symbolism -just as we, the earthlings, identify and classify one another in our everyday life. The alphabets constituting a name have phonetic strength and each has its own wave length or frequency. In modern Numerology, we widely use ENGLISH language alphabets because the ancient seers foresaw them to be concise, complete and correct. So, this system of "Kabala" (means "received from God") numerical values assigned to the letters of a Name along with their mysticism will be dealt with at length in the following pages.

Interestingly, the historic pointers indicate that this art of predicting one's life through numbers and names trace their roots in India. The ancient seers had kept this wisdom as a closely guarded secret, though the spreading and sharing of knowledge was inevitable in later days. Babylonians, Greeks (thanks to the invaluable services of Pythagoras!) Egyptians and Chinese - all had a share of nourishing and codifying it. The Western scholars, who were widely using the Roman script in their languages, did their part of service by scientifically codifying Numerology in such a simple way that even a layman understood the rudiments. The modern practitioners like Sepharial, "Cheiro" and the last but not the least - Pandit Sethuraman of Madras, all gave a status to this science and helped multitudes of humanity that yearned for understanding the course of their lives and improving them. Thus, Numerology was born again!

The findings mentioned by me in this book, "My Fortune" are based on Chaldean system of numbers which had been thoroughly researched into and practiced by my illustrious father Pandit Sethuraman for five decades. It was only the Pandit who proved to the world for the first time that predictions for 108 name numbers could be given with astonishing accuracy and a change in the spelling of one's name could lead to a remarkable change in his or her fortune. The secret of success lies in choosing the right name with the right numbers. In this regard, the Chaldean System proves to be better than any other system as my experience of twenty five years says.

This book, aptly entitled "My Fortune" actually explains the hidden meaning of your Name numbers with reference to Birth and Destiny numbers. Briefly speaking, it unleashes the mysteries of the interplay of the Free will and Fate and teaches you how to succeed in life just by causing appropriate changes in the spelling of your name, if need be. Suggestions regarding lucky names to choose, lucky dates to start a new venture, lucky partners for your business, lucky gemstones to wear are aplenty in this book. Special attention is paid to the subject of love and marriage which feature is scientifically discussed. What and whom to avoid to lead a trouble-free and successful life is also thoroughly explained.

The treasure house of life is full of mysteries. To open its lock which has a set of complicated levers, you do need a 'mystic' key and it is "My Fortune". Use it and you are in not only for surprises, but also SUCCESS!

The mystic key is in your hand and you only need to learn how to open the treasure trove of fortune!

V.S. Guruswamy

WELCOME TO THE WONDERLAND OF FORTUNE!

It is a delightful experience to explain the basics of Numerology to our readers. This branch of predictive science classify the humankind into 9 main categories viz. 9 single numbers starting from 1 representing the 9 planets in the solar system which influence the activities on the earth. They are

$$1 - \text{SUN}$$
$$2 - \text{MOON}$$
$$3 - \text{JUPITER}$$
$$4 - \text{URANUS}$$
$$5 - \text{MERCURY}$$
$$6 - \text{VENUS}$$
$$7 - \text{NEPTUNE}$$
$$8 - \text{SATURN}$$
$$9 - \text{MARS}$$

Suppose a person was born on the 14th March, 1879, (written in figures) = 14-3-1879

(a)   Add the Date numbers; 1+4 = 5 Birth Number **(Mercury)**

(b)   Total = 1+4 + 3 + 1+8 + 7 + 9 = 33 (add again) = 6   Destiny Number **(Venus)**

Birth Number denotes a person's physique, personality traits, inborn qualities, and outlook of life. In short, Birth number signifies the person's image in his/her own view.

Destiny Number denotes how the person looks like in others' view, the current of his destiny and the maximum limit upto which he / she can progress.

Judging a person's life numerologically is to be done by ascertaining the resultant strength and interaction of both birth and destiny numbers and also name numbers.

WHAT'S IN A NAME?

As discussed earlier, each letter of the 26 alphabets of English language is assigned a number with a sound value (The tables as per Chaldean Numerology which we follow is given below). The total compound number in 2 digits or 3 digits decides **how best the person whose Name Number in question uses the cosmological forces of the planet represented by the name which modifies, retards, or accelerates the course of destiny.** The learned readers will now understand that while they cannot change their dates of birth (Fate), they can very well increase or decrease the good / bad effects of their Names (Free will) by causing a change in their names!

CHALDEAN SYSTEM OF NUMBERS

A, I, J, Q, Y	= 1	E, H, N, X	= 5
B, K, R	= 2	U, V, W	= 6
C, G, L, S,	= 3	O, Z	= 7
D, M, T	= 4	F, P	= 8

AN EXAMPLE:

```
A L B E R T        E I N S T E I N
1 3 2 5 2 4        5 1 5 3 4 5 1 5
-----------        ----------------
    17      +       29       =     46
```

(under SUN's influence)

Date of Birth 14th March, 1879 i.e. 14.3.1879

14 = 1+4 = 5. Birth Number is that of MERCURY

1 +4 + 3 + 1 +8 + 7 + 9 = 33 = 6. Destiny Number is that of VE-
NUS

• Einstein was born on 14.3.1879 (March 14, 1879)   = 5 & 6

• Married Mileva Maric, a fellow mathematician in 1901   = 2

(we need not discuss about it for obvious reasons)

• Became Director of Kaiser Wilhelm Research Institute   = 6

(after getting a Ph.D. in Berlin 1914, the same year)

• Submitted his Theory of Relativity in the year 1920   = 3

(6 & 3 are of conflicting vibrations; so his theory helped the scientists
only to invent Atom bomb!)

• Receives 1921 Nobel Prize for Physics in 1922   = 5

• Fled to America fearing Nazi persecution in 1932   = 6

• Died in Princeton, N.J. on 18.4.1955   = 9&6

(For more details about Birth, Destiny and Compound Name numbers, read "SCIENCE OF FORTUNE" and learn yourself numerologically
the lives of 'Men of Destiny". Keep in mind the role of numbers in Einstein's life as explained above).

WHY DO WE JUDGE A NATIVE BY BIRTH, DESTINY AND NAME NUMBERS?

The necessity of analysing someone's life, be it any day he was born
on, is based on the fact that it is only the mutual interaction of the said three
numbers that determines everything about the person and his life. What the
person is endowed with, how far he could go in the life's race for success
and how best he would shine in his endeavours are the three questions
answered by Birth, Destiny and Name numbers. The combined effect of
the Birth and Destiny numbers can be modified by altering the sum total of
the Name Numbers which is achieved by changing the spelling of the name
numerologically. Well, only an enlightened and experienced Numerologist
can do that because it is a "minefield"! If you tread on it carefully avoiding
the "mines", it is fine! Otherwise.....! Quacks in this field have not only

brought disaster to their gullible clients but also discredit to this wonderful science as well!

Before visiting the "knowledge bank" of Numbers and what they portend to mankind, the readers should know a very important point. Just as there is day or night on this earth, there is also a positive or negative "swing" to the power of Numbers - in other words, radiation of energy from the relevant planet. **The good and bad of the native of any number (planet) depends upon this "swing" (radiation) only.** You cannot see Ether but you believe that radio waves travel through it! You cannot see the Rontgen rays, but you are able to see the diagnostic X-ray! This is the age of "cloning" of even humans, but the modern science, though advanced unbelievably, is yet to understand and identify the power of cosmological forces, not to speak of interpreting them!

In the ensuing chapters, I shall be happy to share the secrets of the basic Numbers and their variants.

NUMBER 1 - SUN

The father of the planets in the solar family, the Sun is also the power house and prime mover that activates the animal and plant life on our earth. It gives the life force to all the other planets in the system and the radiations of energy of various planets on us are very much influenced by that of Sun. Just as the Sun which is indispensable to the family of planets and the earthly life, the Number 1 people who are born under the influence of Sun (born on the 1st, 10th, 19th and 28th) are also an important class of their own kind. Avoiding the astronomical logic and astrological mysticism (which are meant for advanced study), you can simply believe that Number 1 people play an important role in all the fields they venture into.

When they are under the positive effect of radiation, they become ambitious, influential and achieve impossible goals. As their category implies, they always want to become "Number 1" in any field of activity and reach respectable levels of authority by the sheer force of their discipline, personality, intellect or good managerial capabilities. They are steadfast in their decisions and hardly back out from them. Love of freedom and hard work, uprightness, capacity to command others, dislike for restraints and interference, religious zeal, willingness to take responsibility, consciousness about their superiority. Love for new ideas and novel plans are some salient features of their positive character. They shine in politics, planetary sciences, travel business, and jobs connected to heat or light. When the influence of sun is negative, Number 1 people become spendthrifts, easily irritable, impatient, irreligious, unrepenting for their mistakes, cruel to their subordinates and quarrelsome. They tend to forget their basic traits like optimism, friendliness, co-operative nature and the inborn magnetism. The negative vibrations may bring about a loss in position, shame in public life, hatred from those placed under them, dissolution of partnerships (or even marriage!), change of job or place and sometimes a revolutionary attempt to change a system or organisation.

What the Birth Dates signify

■ **Date – 1**   Independence or individuality is their watchword. This sometimes causes friction in their relations with others who deal with them. But their sheer doggedness and single-minded devotion takes them to heights of fame (or even notoriety, if the destiny or name numbers are not harmonious!). Their middle age poses some peculiar problems and might retard their progress or force them to change their plans sometimes, or even change residence or office premises. If they are capable of exploiting the weaknesses of their adversaries or rivals, success is assured. Those who are born on the first day of any month will find in the later years of life that they should have had a contingency plan as well. Not much trouble is anticipated for those who are employed for monetary consideration. There may be some slump in the regular income or fame for those in the fields of art or theatre. With a little more adaptability and tolerance they can be happy souls.

■ **Date - 10**   However small or insignificant circle in which these people may be born, they are bound to gradually become popular and command respect. They are more cautious before involving themselves in any venture. They do not sacrifice their money or peace of mind for nothing. The way they handle opposition or challenges in life is a lesson to those who aspire to become successful. Art, literature and of course, politics seem to be of interest to them, but their interest cannot be limited to one particular field alone.

There is a streak of friendliness in their nature. But they are careful in avoiding those who try to exploit them. Sometimes, they are on the difficult walk of life or not-so favourable side of the game in public life. But then, that is their own choice to which they do justice! Other than the routine job they do, whatever it could be, they have interests that are peculiar and not connected to their regular routine. The negative "Swing" of this date may be aggravated by wrong name numbers and the harm that follows is enormous. Greed is their enemy and must be avoided at all costs.

■ Date - 19   Those born on this date have two sides to their personality. Either they could be self-effacing persons with sacrificial tendencies or they could be revolutionaries who have a strong opinion about anything or any person. They generally have strong constitution and take risk in some fields which others may not venture into. Even as writers, artists, or theatre personalities, they exhibit a trait which surprises others, but the latter cannot even imitate them! Their love life sometimes undergoes a jolt, but a strong and unafflicted name number helps it survive, as could be seen in many cases. In public life and in business, their ability to survive storms is legendary. But when things go wrong despite their good efforts, they either totally withdraw or resort to unusual or extreme solutions to escape the onslaught of time. Of all the dates adding up to 1 the 19th born seem to be more versatile, provided their name numbers are in harmony. As for choosing the life partner, caution is necessary, especially when they go in for a relation with number 1 people.

■ Date - 28   This is one of the interesting birth dates, as a good number of people born on this date have some kind of magnetism which they may exploit for their own benefit or for the welfare of the public. In general, they talk to the hearts of those whom they come across and achieve their goal. It is believed that they take calculated risks in life, though at times, they happen to be foolhardy and tip the apple cart. In any field other than politics a good number of people born on the 28th achieve greatness more easily, partly due to their hard work and innate ability to attract others or impress their benefactors. Sometimes, they follow the policy of "Ou Phrontis" (who cares...?) and suffer a pitfall. But, all the same, their capacity to "swim across the current" keeps them afloat. Many of them leave a legacy which may be cherished by the posterity or sometimes in different circumstances, even despised strongly. However, their impact on the society cannot be forgotten. They may be ambitious but must ensure that avarice on their part does not lead to disaster!

People born under Birth Number 1 (born on the 1st, 10th, 19th and 28th of any month) and with various Destiny Numbers will find their lives as follows:

BIRTH NUMBER 1 & DESTINY NUMBER 1 (SUN – SUN)

They are ruled by Sun in the real sense which means they are the people in Number 1 series who come under the total influence of Sun. Very enterprising that they are, they are also known for their stubbornness and unchangeable desires. The quality of asserting themselves in any situation, proving their authority even when not necessary, creativeness in their approach, sometimes over-optimism, paying more attention to the weaknesses of employees or servants placed under them (to some extent, family members also!), habit of mechanically applying their sense of discipline unmindful of the results, dominating in love or marital affairs, thirst for introducing new systems or off-beat ideas and beginning a venture (or adventure!) in a foreign country are the basic traits of this combination. It is a matter of interest that grudgingly or otherwise, people obey or follow them!

When positively disposed, 1 & 1 people are good achievers. Otherwise, they are the most hated lot, drifting from place to place and shifty in their views and relations.

★ **Newsmakers of 1 & 1:**
Auguste Lumiére
Andrei N. Tupolev
James watt
Martin Luther
Salman Rushdie
Dhirubhai Ambani

NUMBER 1 - SUN
BIRTH NUMBER 1 & DESTINY NUMBER 2 (SUN - MOON)

This class of people, if having positive vibrations of the planet is good at any work connected to public relations. Generally, they marry people richer and more influential than themselves. Industries and jobs connected to drinks, fluids, travels, sometimes even religion or law offers good opportunities to them. Women under this combination take unusual decisions, which, when positive give an astounding success. They are successful in hiding their feelings, secret love affairs and are capable of tiding over many a difficult situation in their lives. Voyages, shipping business, writing investigative reports, activities connected to secret organizations, alchemy and the like offer them fair chances to shine. When it comes to managing a business or wear the mantle of gubernatorial posts, these people are more articulate and clever even when their public image is tarnished. Generally, they prove to be materially successful and more acceptable than their 1 & 1 counterparts because they are more cooperative in difficult circumstances.

When 1 & 2 happens to be a businessman (or business woman) the life becomes somewhat "balanced." Though the person takes a strong view of how things should be, during the course of action some flexibility may be seen.

If the Destiny Number 2 is of negative vibration, the person confuses himself and starts vacillating. The rigid decisions already taken, especially in noble projects or humanitarian work suffers towards the end. A similar situation arises even in the married life also. Any kind of relation, alliance or partnerships involving Birth & Destiny Numbers 1 & 2 respectively is successful, provided the person ventures away from his or her birth place or chooses an "off-beat" profession attracting public attention. This person needs an important advice - "Do not use a hammer to kill a fly!".

★ Newsmakers of **1** & **2**:

Jacqueline Kennedy Onassis

Bill Clinton

Edgar Allan Poe

Omar Sharif

P.V. Narasimha Rao

Dom Moraes

BIRTH NUMBER 1 & DESTINY NUMBER 3 (SUN - JUPITER)

This is a harmonious combination. The person who has 1 & 3 numbers are bound to achieve things considered "impossible" by others. Positively speaking, the foolhardy nature of Number 1 or the impulsiveness in actions remain well balanced by 3 which gives discipline, calculativeness, the capacity to "foresee" things, the power of speech combined with self-assertion and they all play into one's life and help him climb the ladder of fame. Though successful in politics and labour relations, if "over-suspicious" nature surfaces in the mind (there is every possibility!), everything comes to a standstill! That's the point to be clearly understood by the people under this number to avoid mishaps in life. Interesting personalities are born under this combination and those who achieved great goals in their lives enjoyed the benefit of their achievement only when they did **not** act overconfidently! Even in the lowest strata of life, the 1 & 3 persons leave their dent in whichever sphere they dwell in.

If negatively disposed, the persons born under 1 & 3 combination become victims of their own virtues. They become egoistic, sometimes even eccentric, over-religious, biased in their views, impulsive in action (for which they repent later!) and waste their energy in regrouping all the forces or resources at their disposal towards the end of their lives. However, they are sure to acquire lasting fame or notoriety!

NUMBER 1 - SUN

★ Newsmakers of **1** & **3**:

Joseph Heller

Indira Gandhi

Irving Wallace

Kurt Gödel

Boris Pasternak

Charles G.Koch

BIRTH NUMBER 1 & DESTINY NUMBER 4 (SUN - URANUS)

These people present a numerologically interesting combination since Sun and Uranus are of opposite characters. But the person under Numbers 1 & 4 helps others, especially those who may not even agree with their views. They achieve a lot in a field, sometimes totally unconnected to their childhood background. Even their married lives seem to be somewhat stranger than those of others. If they avoid or postpone marriage, then their latent powers work fully well in their profession, (which secret is perplexing!) The magnetic vibrations which may be equated with the mutual attraction of opposite poles carry their message to the world in a forceful way! Their victories give them long-lasting fame and positions, but defeats make them totally a non-entity. The salient feature of this combination of Sun-Uranus is that they are capable of attracting "masses". The positive trait of these persons will be their organising capacity that makes others wonder as to how well they plan and execute . Thus they become indispensable to the society! The positively "swung" combination of 1 and 4 leaves legacies to the world they live in, their service to humanity sometimes remaining unexcelled by many others in their sphere of life.

If under negative "Swing" or vibrations, the persons under 1 & 4 combination become an antagonist, a dictator, sometimes deeply involved in litigation, and some other time, betrayed by their own companions or partners. At least, some of them are bound to cause some political upheavals at some point of their career.

19

★ Newsmakers of 1 & 4:

Dr. Annie Besant

Dr. D.S.Kotnis

Bill Gates

Mrs. Wallis Simpson

Nicolas Sarkozy

Pamela Anderson

BIRTH NUMBER 1 & DESTINY NUMBER 5 (SUN - MERCURY)

These persons think faster, decide faster, and organise faster than people of any other combinations. They are respected by people from all walks of life (but not by a few born under 1 or 8 - sometimes!) They have good knowledge about the world and its people and materially they become successful if they exploit their public relations. Otherwise, they become recluses or hermits or even revolutionaries. They expect things to move fast and the self-assertive nature of Number 1 and the stimulating vibrations of Number 5, if interacting positively, take them to lofty heights in whichever field they are in. This 1-5 combination is peculiar in its own way, because unlike other combinations this takes its natives to unknown destinations or fields and also helps them shine. Inheriting a property or a legacy unexpectedly may happen in their lives. Sometimes, they venture into a business which may not be their cup of tea! But the organising capacity of Number 1 and the universal adaptability of Number 5 reveal dazzling prospects to them. Either their bodies or minds **must** keep "journeying" always; if not, the full force of 1 & 5 is considered absent in their destiny. Honours and benefits from government come by themselves.

The negative "swing" of this 1 & 5 combination is harmful to the family life. Blood relatives cause a lot of anxiety and either they themselves or their compatriots in politics put these people in trouble one way or the other. The situation worsens only when the Numbers of such people are antagonistic.

★ Newsmakers of 1 & 5:
Samuel Hahnemann
Javier Perez De Cuellar
King Birendra Bikram Shah
Liv Tyler
Aishwarya Rai
Amancio Ortega Gaona

BIRTH NUMBER 1 & DESTINY NUMBER 6 (SUN - VENUS)

Be it any field the Number 1 & 6 people are placed, they have their way! The leadership qualities of Number 1 combined with the hard work and planning skill, if well-matched with the talents and the bewitching manners and beauty of the Destiny Number 6, then there is nothing that they cannot achieve in this world! Most of the people born under this combination find initially that their lives are paths of thorns. But soon they realise that they could be "beds of roses" also and that they are in for very great achievements. To achieve, however, they need a **"catalyst"** which may come to them in any form [Not discussing individual lives, we can derive this fact out of the Birth and Destiny Numbers (1&6) of Sri Ramakrishna Mission or introduction of EURO, which serve as a couple of examples to cite] Whether politics, religion or fine arts or even an unknown field, their magnetism transcends all barriers, provided they avoid self-defeatist attitude.

There is also a negative side to their numbers. 1 & 6 combination makes them blind to the harsh realities of life. Even if they are successful, they fail to enjoy fully the benefits of their labour. They become self-admirers unwittingly and cause agony to themselves or they tend to torture others. Their charms, intelligence, fruits of labour all disappear one day, but the fame remains!

★ Newsmakers of **1 & 6**:

Count Louis Hamon ("CHEIRO")

Rudy Giuliani

Ho Chi Minh

Sister Nivedita

Meena Kumari

Dr.Satyendranath Bose

BIRTH NUMBER 1 & DESTINY NUMBER 7
(SUN - NEPTUNE)

These two numbers, one conflicting other's vibrations have only one rule to follow to become successful. The positive aspects of Number 1&7, viz. intuitiveness, imagining things even beyond the reach of fantasy, the romantic disposition, god fearing nature, philosophical approach, inquisitiveness, love for varieties, and inventions or discoveries, interest in social service or religion and thirst for literary achievement - all put together, will carry them to enviable heights. It is the hands of Destiny that does not always bestow benign vibrations in this case, surprisingly, even in married life!

The positive qualities discussed above may sometimes fail and the life and achievements come to a grinding halt. Either they become ascetics or recluses or "vanish into the thin air" one day. Such disappointing events occur even in their married life. They are feared, hated or left in the lurch, because in spite of Number 1 being the Birth Number, the people of this combination either overplay or underplay the cards of their lives. Their impractical attitude towards the people who are close to them or over - confidence in their capabilities, lands them in trouble. However, those who are bestowed with good Name Numbers or those who "exploit" the vibrations of good Numbers of dates they choose, are monumentally successful. They become legends even after their death and those with the positive "swing" of this combination of numbers are remembered by posterity for even centuries to come!

NUMBER 1 - SUN

★ Newsmakers of **1 & 7**:

Princess Diana
Antonio Banderas
John Edgar Hoover
Harold MacMillan
Marilyn Monroe
Joseph Pulitzer
Saddam Hussein

BIRTH NUMBER 1 & DESTINY NUMBER 8 (SUN - SATURN)

Since the faculties of Number 1 (Sun) and those of 8 (Saturn) are opposite, the person represented by this combination could be an admixture of conflicting interests and habits. The love for power is sometimes satisfied by hook or crook. Early separation, -natural or otherwise from spouse, short-lived business partnerships, secretly or openly rebellious activities (there is no policy of moderation!) suspicious nature and reckless business ventures or autocratic administration are certain characteristics of this 1 & 8 combination. If they are successful in any walk of life (You may even find them in the profession of Law!), it only means that the aforesaid qualities had a "positive swing" which helped them achieve their goals. In other words, the Name Numbers or the dates of their endeavours could have been favourable which caused a sense of moderation in their outlook.

It is not surprising that these people become popular (in the strictest sense,-notorious!) when it comes to the question of politics or religion, if the negative vibrations predominate. They cause a lot of harm to the society or country they live in and they do not mind to shed blood (it need not be theirs!) or sacrifice lives. With the same combination of Birth & Destiny Numbers, people with positive vibrations have espoused the cause of their countries and friends and have been "immortalised" by history. Yet, there is always a grave side to their nature!

★ **Newsmakers of 1 & 8:**

Nathuram Vinayak Godse

Osama Bin Laden

John Wilkes Booth

Boris Yeltsin

Aung San Suu Kyi

Jonas Salk

BIRTH NUMBER 1 & DESTINY NUMBER 9 (SUN - MARS)

Under Number 1 series, 1 & 9 offers the best combination. When No.1 people plan and direct, No.9 people execute scrupulously. In any walk of life, the persons under this category use their brains and brawns as well and create a kind of sensation. They knowingly face challenges and risks and their success depends upon their Name Numbers and favourable dates chosen for execution of their plans. Scientists, actors or musicians, doctors, politicians or even writers or priests -be it any one, they introduce revolutionary ideas which appeal to the public. Hard work is the hallmark of their character. They are sometimes mistaken for their strange beliefs and habits but their service to whatever cause they espouse cannot be forgotten. Service by exerting themselves physically or by way of money or proper advice is always available from them. Facing risk or opposition in the course of their action in any field is not a strange or stray incident in their life. The pity is that when they leave this world, they would be strongly feeling that their work or service has remained incomplete. Positive thinking or healthy grooming will help the children of this category to become useful to the society or country, but lack of patriotism or social cause will make them antisocial. That is why under this group you will find either famous surgeons who save the lives of their patients or notorious terrorists or extremists (Both use knives as tools of their trade!). In politics or public life, it is a common phenomenon that you find these people either as socially conscious philanthropists or donors or as corrupt (even morally) "swindlers". Most of them, be it any category or sex, find their married life difficult. However, all of them are "achievers"!

★ Newsmakers of **1** & **9**:
Jean-Francois Gravelet
Nicolaus Copernicus,
E.M.Forster
G.D.Birla
Mukesh Ambani
Sir Thomas J. Lipton

NAME NUMBERS AND THEIR INTERPRETATIONS

If the sum total of the values of letters in your name adds upto Number 1, then you are under domination of the Number 1, which represents the planet SUN. When the date of birth or the destiny number falls under 1, 4 or 8, the name number under No. 1 will bestow full benefits. If people born under other numbers have names under Number 1, they may progress in life but their life will be fraught with problems and turbulence. One must study the characteristics of letters in the names and their corresponding numbers to know their effects in full.

■ Name No. **10**: This number when comes as a name indicates the sound or resonance of the primal force. This is depicted in the ancient texts as a snake enmeshed within a wheel. Those named under this number will be dignified and popular. Confidence and patience co-exist in their lives but their fortunes will change frequently. It is like a revolving wheel, with frequent ups and downs. They must be honest in all their activities and they are bound to gain popularity. They will lead happy lives since there will be no paucity of funds.

■ Name No.**19**: Ancient books on this subject attribute mastery over the Three Worlds to this Number and as such, these people will be the focus of attention wherever they are. This number indicates the Rising Sun. This also has been described as the "Prince of the Celestial World" in ancient Indian texts and as an "Ideal Lover" in Egyptian scriptures. The sun becomes brighter as the day lengthens and so also these people progress as their age advances. Position, status, happiness, success and

25

wealth will be gradually on the rise. Being well-disciplined, they will look young and will be very active even in their advanced age. They must be honest even in matters related to sensual pleasures.

■ **Name No.28**: Those with this name number do progress and get all the comforts during the early part of life but they frequently face struggles or difficulties in all their endeavours in life. They may have to start their lives again and again always afresh, many times over. Although they progress very fast in their lives, they finally lose everything due to the cruel stroke of fate. One of the examples of such people born under this number is General MacArthur, a fine soldier who deserved more of honour and recognition, but was deprived of his position and career by President Truman of USA! Those coming under this number may incur unexpected losses due to their friends and relatives. Money lent by them rarely comes back. As such, this number can only be regarded as an unlucky one, since all the hard-earned money may be lost unexpectedly.

■ **Name No.37**: This is a very lucky number. It will lift even an ordinary person to the most prominent positions in life. It brings success in love and the patronage of the elite. These people will have good friends from both sexes. They will be greatly favoured by men if they are women and vice versa. As a result, their lives will improve greatly. People will come forward to invest their capital with such people. Accumulation of money and wealth will be easy through various means. They will have an active interest in the fine arts and in all probability, lead comfortable and luxurious lives. They will be renowned for their pleasing manners and countenance. Some of them will be philanderers because of their casual attitude towards opposite sex. This number, which gives unexpected success, is a desirable one.

(Note: If people who occupy very high positions have their names under this number, it may bring them unnecessary problems. This number will bring good fortune to ordinary people. These people should remain satisfied when they attain a certain position in life and should not be too ambitious. This number, will bring fortune automatically, but will lose its power when one becomes too greedy.)

NUMBER 1 - SUN

■ **Name No.46:** This has been described as the "Crowned Head" in the ancient texts. It means that when prudence, intelligence and knowledge are used wisely, it will bring the crown of life. Whatever may be the business, this number will help one to reach the pinnacle of success and is capable of raising even the most ordinary person to the position of a ruler. Wealth and status will go up with the advancement of age. People belonging to this number should be honest in all walks of life.

■ **Name No.55:** This number predicts that both creation and destruction can be done by a single power. This will bring victory over enemies. Before entering the battlefield, Greek soldiers were ordered to wear a talisman marked with number 55 around their necks. This number is the epitome of will-power and intuition. People under this number will astonish others by their knowledge and win them over. They are acknowledged as scholars. Wisdom and intelligence will be as bright as lightning. If not used in a proper way, this may destroy them. Knowledge in various subjects could be acquired by those born under this number.

■ **Name No. 64** This number will create equal number of friends and foes. Opposition will be experienced in life. This gives extraordinary will power, intelligence and knowledge. This will bestow fame by enabling them to do things that are considered impossible. This ensures high position in the Government. At times, this will give such a high position that everyone will pay respect and hold these people in high esteem and awe. Their words would cast a powerful influence.

■ **Name No. 73:** This name number strengthens mental faculties and bestows fame, wealth and power. People having this number will aspire to lead comfortable lives and will accomplish their desires. Support from the people of authority will be available and material possessions will be in plenty. If they are not honest, they will lose their fame. If they are the spiritual types, they will lead a peaceful and comfortable life with pure hearts and noble thoughts.

MY FORTUNE

■ **Name No. 82:** This is one of the most powerful numbers and it can elevate even an ordinary person to the status of a ruler. Those having this number in their names are duty-conscious. With unceasing efforts, they will dominate the scene in any field they are placed in. They would own lands, gold mines and precious gems. They are lovers of high-bred horses and will attain the pinnacle of fame by making a fortune either in horse races, car races or in similar sports or business. They create unnecessary problems in their love matters and will be over-adamant in nature. Their eyes have magnetic powers. If the power of this number is properly understood and practiced, no physical or mental feat is impossible to perform.

■ **Name No. 91:** This indicates strong determination and profitable journeys. They also undertake many journeys for trade or otherwise and will do all things with great vigour. Maritime trade using boats and ships will bring them plenty of wealth. They can attain success in yogic exercises like meditation or concentration. Comfortable living awaits them.

■ **Name No. 100:** Even though this number is capable of giving success in all efforts, it will not offer many opportunities. There will be plenty of money. This number implies a long and comfortable life, without any major achievements.

LOVE AND MARRIAGE

Unlike the pre-historic human beings, the modern men and women have a definite Code of conduct as far as the subjects of love and marriage are concerned. Love denotes the natural and basic instinct for companionship between a man and a woman. When it culminates in an affectionate partnership of attachment, it is called marriage which is the most civilised institution of human life. These subtle feelings of our routine life are based on mutual vibrations and compatibility, which, in the numerological parlance, are called "harmonious numbers" or "disharmonious numbers". It only means that the birth, destiny and name numbers of the couple are SUITABLE for a healthy, sustaining and productive relation or NOT. It is a proven fact that the planetary influences on each of us decide the emotional and physical health and also the type of person we must choose to love or marry. And this is the secret, "My Fortune" wants everyone of you to understand, so that your love life or married life remains peaceful and hassle-free!

FOR THOSE BORN ON THE 1st, 10th, 19th AND 28th OF ANY MONTH

Sun is your planet. He is the Lord of the solar family. Like him, you also think you are the master of your personal or professional life. You are powerful, active and independent but you forget at times that there are occasions during which you suffer "eclipse"!

Your Number is 1 and it vibrates favourably to those born on the 4th and 8th series of dates. There is considerable degree of mutual attraction. Marriage will be favourable. If name numbers are also lucky, you are well suited to each other.

It is possible that those born on the 2nd, 3rd, 5th, 6th and their series of dates may be passive to you in love or marriage, though the suitability may not be at its best.

You are advised not to involve deeply with or commit yourself to those born on the dates of 1st, 7th or 9th and their series. Their vibes disagree with yours and hence their company may not be suited for a long term relation. But, in a few cases the relationship survives, because of favourable name numbers which give you a lot of diplomacy.

MISCELLANY

People born under Number 1 should choose 1st, 10th, 19th of any month to commence auspicious endeavours. It is better to avoid 28th. Dates 8, 17 and 26 are not favourable (especially 26th of any month). On 4th, 13th, 22nd or 31st of any month, they may expect favourable results unexpectedly.

Gold is their lucky metal and Ruby is their lucky stone. In colors, yellow is the most suitable. Even any other light colours are favourable. It is better to avoid black or dark brown.

NUMBERS AND NEWS :

Snails have sex only once in their lifetime; it prolongs for more than 12 hours!

NUMBER 2 - MOON

People born on the 2nd, 11th, 20th and 29th of any month and / or those with Destiny Numbers (the sum total of the numbers in one's date of birth) totalling to the single number 2 are ruled by the Number 2 (Moon). Just as the moon which waxes and wanes, they are also people of many moods. One moment they are warm and affectionate and the next moment they become cold and aloof. Generally, they reflect the situations in which they are placed. Imagination, psychic ability, clairvoyance, poetic skill, thirst for learning unknown secrets, inclination to fine arts, computing skills, proficiency in games involving brain work, cinema or stage are the foundations of their character. Even if they are found in the fields not acceptable to the society (due to negative vibrations of Number 2 or planet Moon), still they employ the skills and talents of the positive nature mentioned above. Interestingly, this category consists of people from all kinds of profession or vocation. The reason is that they are capable of capturing others' attention by appealing to their sensitivities and moods. This can be compared to our liking the moonlight more than the scorching sunlight! If these Number 2 people can overcome their fickle-mindedness and lethargy and exercise utmost concentration in what they do, sky is the limit of their success!

MY FORTUNE

What the Birth Dates signify

■ **Date - 2** Those born on 2nd day of any month in general, possess vivid imagination and thinking power. But when they decide to act, it has to be always result-oriented. They believe in the maxim, "Pen is mightier than sword!" and express their opinion frankly through their speeches or writing. Some people born on this date tend to become religious leaders, though it is not always the case and at one stage of their career they are criticised for their views. In art, literature or in entertainment industry, they are rather successful. In other fields, though they might become legends, yet there is always a streak of melancholy added to their lives. Interestingly, they try to relish it and thus become an enigma to others who observe them with curiosity. Many among them become popular in far away countries or societies where they might become role models also. They may at times cause embarrassment to their close associates, not to exclude even their own kith and kin. It is simply due to the fact that those born on the 2nd of any month are more open-minded and think only about the "ultimate" and not about the "immediate"! When they grow in status, they better avoid being egoistic. They would soon learn that such an advice would pay rich dividends!

■ **Date - 11** Those who are born on the 11th of any month generally possess aesthetic sense and express their thoughts in unequivocal language. You may find many of them pursuing religion seriously, but at the same time a good number of them being die-hard rationalists or atheists also. Some people born on this date become famous inventors and sports stars, though physical prowess alone need not be the criterion. At one stage or the other, religion or god tends to play an important role in their lives and even in such cases they accept the doctrine only after careful study and contemplation. Some people become examples for "rags - to - riches" story and such cases are, of course, exceptions. If those born on the 11th are following devious or dubious methods to become rich or famous, –ironically enough, they do win, but not without some personal losses. What helps most of them to emerge successful in the game of life is that they have an innate ability to read the thoughts of their adversaries and those around them. Anyhow, some who lack this ability do succumb to their fate, meet with disappointments, and could be at loggerheads with law at times. They learn sooner or later that they could improve their fortunes, if they do not injure others' feelings. Their greatest strength lies in understanding the truth, that by helping others they help themselves.

■ Date - 20 Those born on the 20th of any month evoke interest of the people who venture into the subject of Numerology. People with positive name numbers liberate the mankind from sufferings by their teachings, writings and actions. Others become dreaded characters. But both the lots do change the course of history or influence the minds of those who follow them or believe them. That is why we find these people in the group of saints and in the group of sinners as well. Good destiny number and harmonious name number provide great spiritual strength to those born on the 20th and make them contribute positively to the welfare of mankind. Whatever category they may belong to, they are crowd-pullers and it needs a lot of intelligence on the part of those who judge them good or bad. What is more mysterious in their personality is that they espouse a cause which is either really noble or "seems" to be noble. The history really owes a reply to the posterity as to how the 20th born people shape its course, in spite of innumerable challenges and trials in their life or career. There is an unknown fear lurking in their minds leading to suspicion at times and the result is anybody's guess!

■ Date – 29 In a struggle for success, in a battle for supremacy or in achieving one's goal in the routine life of challenges, you must have observed a handful of people who hardly give up their fight till the end. Their purpose may be noble or evil but "get going" is their policy. If bad associations or bad aims in their life influence them, they do a lot of harm to the society in which they live; otherwise, their service to the mankind becomes legendary. It all depends upon the positive or negative name numbers or destiny numbers. At times, some of them feel the grip of law at their throats and unlike many others, these people stoically face the situation. Their spirit of enterprise is unparalleled and with favourable destiny and name numbers, they become admirable personalities in their second half of lifetime. There is always a secret side to their nature and activities and a kind of "roller coaster" experience in their love life or marriage is not ruled out, if other factors like destiny and name numbers are not harmonious. Some such relations may also lead to disaster. Interestingly, some of these people achieve success at a very young age in the field of writing or histrionics, but find it difficult to enjoy fully the fruits of their success due to the cruel stroke of destiny. The early texts and experienced foretellers deal with this birth number forthrightly citing some negative qualities, though such qualities are mitigated or nullified by favourable destiny and name numbers. First of all, they should cultivate the habit of doing good to people around themselves.

Because of the ominous nature of this number 29, those born on this date or those whose name numbers add up to 29 are advised not to choose 29th of any month for conducting auspicious ceremonies, for holding important functions or for signing or registering important documents. (We do not lose anything by avoiding this date, but may gain immensely by choosing a luckier date). If only did they cast away the negative traits in their character, they would bring honour to themselves and the society or organisation they belong to!

People born under Birth Number 2 (born on the 2nd, 11th, 20th and 29th of any month) and with various Destiny Numbers will find their lives as follows:

BIRTH NUMBER 2 & DESTINY NUMBER 1 (MOON -SUN)

The 2 & 1 combination gives good prospects to those born under its vibrations. In business, this lot finds the going easy. In love, they win others' hearts easily. In politics, religion, cinema or media their impact is stupendous. The reason is that they choose a different "style" of functioning! In business connected to water, oil, exports and also those involving travels they are successful. Generally, these people start in a humble way but come up in a big way. There is something "off-beat" in their nature that distinguishes them from others. In other words, there is always a "mystic" side to their nature. At one stage or the other, these people "rub the Law on the wrong side" and suffer a jolt. They are humorous, of course, but there is a grave side to it which does not permit them to enjoy life fully. In politics or in matters connected to public life, their ideas are forcefully presented and sometimes the same ideas may boomerang on them! But of all the Birth-Destiny Numbers under 2, this is, however a lucky one!

★ Newsmakers of 2 & 1:

Emile Zola
Rajiv Gandhi
Mikhail Gorbachev
Joseph Goebbels
Aristotle Onassis
Rupert Murdoch

BIRTH NUMBER 2 & DESTINY NUMBER 2 (MOON - MOON)

This Number 2 & 2 combination gives an extreme nature and they attract the world's attention by their extreme moral or spiritual supremacy or harsh antagonism. They are either dictators or as sweet as children. Rank rationalists or devout spiritualists, both come under No. 2 & 2 category. Patience, love, forbearance, interest in social causes, passive resistance to oppressive systems, diplomatic approach to problems, love of children and respect for religion are some salient features of their character. Whether positive or negative the vibrations of the combination are, this lot generally finds their spouses depart early. Some, of course, are celibates. A few find their spouses living longer, provided the Name Numbers of both partners are in good harmony or the marriage dates are auspicious numerologically. Even business partnerships survive when each partner innovates in his or her own way but in different theatre of operation. When this "totally lunar" people apply their minds to adventure sports or art or even humanitarian causes, they become "heroes" of their community or nation. The negative vibrations also make them "heroes" alright, but soon they are exposed and branded as "lunatics"!

★ **Newsmakers of 2 & 2:**

Hans Christian Andersen

Steve Waugh

Edmund Hillary

Benito Mussolini

Satyajit Ray

Marquis de Sade

BIRTH NUMBER 2 & DISTINY NUMBER 3
(MOON - JUPITER)

The negative qualities of Moon such as fickle-mindedness, dreaming nature without foreseeing result, hesitation to act and the like are nullified by this combination of 2 & 3.The planet that denotes discipline, confidence, honour and honesty adds more power and the person signified by this Moon - Jupiter partnership goes a long way in pursuits relating to poetry, meditation, computing, Mathematics, and social reforms. Some have occult or religious interests which they follow in their own peculiar way. Medicine, pharmaceuticals, dealing in artifacts or cosmetics and philosophy of a revolutionary nature are certain fields in which they shine. In politics, this combination makes the person shrewd and opportunistic. Though they behave like "time-servers", they are, however, successful! With a "negative swing" of Numbers in the date of birth or in the name, these persons may have a "bad" marriage too. But their choice of spouses born on dates of 1 series or 7 series increases the span of married life and they should marry on dates not antagonistic to their Birth & Destiny numbers. They are tough negotiators so far as their own ends are satisfied. When they are noble, they are wonderful human beings!

The negative traits make them cunning and deceitful. Vanity becomes their watchword and for the sake of comfortable living they sacrifice scruples. They fail to bother about the priorities of life at times.

★ Newsmakers of 2 & 3:

Imelda Marcos

Thomas Paine

J.Krishnamurti

Viswanathan Anand

Jerome K.Jerome

N.R.Narayana Murthy

BIRTH NUMBER 2 & DESTINY NUMBER 4
(MOON – URANUS)

The persons born under this combination of Numbers 2 & 4 are a mixture of both good and bad. If not their character, at least their lives' events prove that fact. The vivid imagination, sense of social-consciousness and aesthetic sense of Number 2 could become a healthy blend with the methodical approach, researching tendencies and scholastic confidence of Number 4. Or otherwise, the coldness, envy and calculative hesitation of Number 2 mixed with the stubbornness, opinionated views over politics or religion may cause embarrassing situations that impede the progress in life or bring loss of image or honour. Success in life depends upon the predominance of good qualities of both the numbers, coupled with a good Name number. In politics or religion or business deals involving money or the world of cinema, at one stage or the other, life becomes very difficult for these people. The wise and the intuitive foresee what would happen and escape destiny by changing or relinquishing the responsibility, but the not-so-shrewd types succumb. (It may be so with their married life also). This bad stroke of luck is avoidable by choosing the right people as companions or partners. But in majority of the cases under this combination, destiny has its way! Under ideal number combination, this 2 & 4 people become idols of worship.

The following are some important personalities born under 2 & 4 series:

    ★ Newsmakers of 2 & 4:
      Johnny Weissmuller
      John Major
      Archbishop Thomas Cranmer
      Rosa Mota
      Harold Wilson
      Gregor Mendel
      Keanu Reeves

BIRTH NUMBER 2 & DESTINY NUMBER 5
(MOON - MERCURY)

Many qualities, such as, skepticism, lethargy, and shyness are overcome by the Destiny Number 5 which is ruled by Mercury. Mercury is a fast-moving planet and is the significator of Wisdom. Though astrologically Mercury is not in healthy tune with Moon, the net result of the combination - if properly used, will bring very good results. You only have to ensure that the Name number is appropriate. There are cases known to me in which Moon (Number 2) helped the people of this combination to "soft pedal" in their investments which averted disaster! If Mercury (Number 5 mostly involves people in business activities) which acts in "haste" had been listened to, a terrific loss would have hit the natives concerned! However, people who have these numbers in their dates of birth should ensure that the dates on which they embark upon new ventures, the dates on which they travel, the numbers of their Names or their business names are numerologically in harmony! If the purpose of their mission is noble, they succeed despite some loss in the bargain. Their achievements also become historic! but if they carry on with their whims and fancies unmindful of the welfare of their country or their own self, doom will surely follow! With a noble ideal and a service-minded attitude these 2 & 5 people are quick to become popular and their community does not forget them also. The "negative" types of people also remain in the memory of the people but for a different reason. In business and in pursuits which appeal to the eyes and ears of the public, they are successful. There is one thing which is commonly found in the lives of 2 & 5 people. They meet with accidents -sometimes often, and they are in the habit of hardly looking back if they have decided to journey. Just as they escape accidents miraculously, they also escape mishaps in their career,-especially politics! But people who are honest and noble do not face such problems. Some of these people who exploit the intuitiveness and industriousness of this combination open up big businesses and shine very well. Some others become either ascetics or revolutionaries. Power in their hands becomes a tool which needs "great care" while handling. It either emancipates the mankind or eliminates it physically! So, positiveness of purpose must be taught to the children of this group while bringing them up. For people or places ruled by Mercury, 2 & 5 dates are not favourable, if the Birth Number is 11 or 29.

★ Newsmakers of 2 & 5:

Andre Agassi

Lord Horatio Nelson

Bobby Charlton

Adolf Hitler

W.E.Gladstne

J.R.D.Tata

BIRTH NUMBER 2 & DESTINY NUMBER 6 (MOON - VENUS)

Imagine how a person would be if he or she has histrionic talents mixed with scholarly reservedness. Such is the rare combination of Numbers 2 (Moon) and 6 (Venus)! Though the persons born under this combination seem to benefit from both the Numbers, 6 or Venusian qualities dominate the psyche of these people. That is why a lot of artistes are born under this numerical alliance. No doubt, there is a fair sprinkle of diplomats and social reformers in this lot, but what is common in all of them is the harmonious blend of magnetism, spontaneous fellowship and glib of the tongue. Money, fanatic followers, skill in fine arts or science - all will find an important place in their lives. When these persons appear in public, people follow them with reverence. Though some of them contribute to the world great philosophic or social ideals, their noble efforts are forgotten after their death. But the worldly lot continues to be "worshipped" despite all the scandals, if any, affecting them. Most of them become answerable to "Law" one day or the other. Their lives become legends, if morality and humanitarian cause become their watchword and such people are born rarely under these numbers. Some of them may be maimed due to the negative vibrations of Moon or disabled but all the same, the world is happy only when the 2 & 6 people prove their presence!

★ **Newsmakers of 2 & 6:**

Salma Hayek

Michael Jackson

Dag Hammarskjold

Romain Rolland

Thomas Alva Edison

BIRTH NUMBER 2 & DESTINY NUMBER 7
(MOON - NEPTUNE)

Numbers 2 and 7 are with mutual affinity as per the numerological findings, though Moon is subject to eclipse. But the persons under this combination seem to "exploit" Number 2 qualities to their benefit reserving their wisdom and enterprising spirit for using on the right day, when needed. The tenacity with which they bear the problems of life is legendary. This is because of the influence of Neptune.

Their mothers or sisters play an important role in these peoples' childhood in majority of the cases. Many thespians, musicians, poets and such others who appeal to the emotions of the public are born under this category. If they are in politics or military, some of them are sure to desert it or undergo imprisonment due to some reason or the other. But Neptune which is considered significator of wisdom strengthens their will power and teaches them how to overcome any hurdles in life. Their spirit of freedom is phenomenal and their psychic power is abnormal. Even those who hate them would secretly appreciate their abilities. When people under other number combinations may need a "catalyst" or a "godfather" to help, this 2 & 7 personalities think, plan, work untiringly and achieve their goals all by themselves. Good or bad, these people are masters of their own destiny. They only need to be careful with the opposite sex.

★ Newsmakers of 2 & 7:

Zubin Mehta

Leonardo Dicaprio

Dhyan Chand

Uri Geller

John F. Kennedy

Slobodan Milosevic

BIRTH NUMBER 2 & DESTINY NUMBER 8
(MOON - SATURN)

It is common knowledge that other than the good or lucky in the world there are some bad elements also. In the same way, among the bad or unlucky, good lives sprout too! This is a mystery of creation which has only a philosophical or metaphysical answer. When individually discussed, the numbers (Birth) 2 and 8 have produced noble or lucky lives on this earth. But the combination of 2 and 8 as Birth and Destiny Numbers respectively warrants deeper study. When the positive qualities of 2 such as, thirst for knowledge, imaginative power, contemplation, introspection, sympathy, love for change and idealism are blended with sense of dutifulness, austerity, love of justice, willingness to work hard and God-fearing nature, wonderful human beings will be born on this earth. Otherwise, religious bigotry, lack of foresight, foolhardy efforts, destructive tendencies and suspicious nature pre-dominate and such people ruin themselves and others around them. Whatever may be the queerness in their views and actions, they have a place in history! It is important that they must choose the right and auspicious day for doing any good work, beneficial to them and their families. The products connected to both Moon and Saturn would be the commodity they deal in, sell or manufacture, such as foundries, moulding works, steel-rolling, drinks, or paints and liquids manufactured with the help of machinery. Some people deal in agricultural products also. Politics and military finally bring gloom to these natives, though they are good strategists and leaders. At the same time, good Name Numbers and prayers have done miracles in the lives of people born under this category as evident from the living examples. One advice that is to be given to people of this combination is that "Be moderate in your approach to problems; save for the rainy day; choose good Name Number and favourable dates to commence work!" (Handle weapons carefully).

★ Newsmakers of 2 & 8:

Lord Robert Clive

Lord Curzon

Patrice Lumumba

Emperor Hirohito

General Patton

Enid Blyton

BIRTH NUMBER 2 & DESTINY NUMBER 9 (MOON - MARS)

Moon and Mars are numerologically neutral to each other. The combined vibrations they set upon 2 & 9 people maybe friendly or inimical depending upon the dates of birth or other astrological data available. In politics they are the driving force to achieve peace. In arts or sports they reach unparalleled heights and also dwell there for long. In professions dealing with chemicals, explosives and tools or weapons they achieve something which others may not! They shed blood or cause others to shed! Not to cite a frightening example, we may say that they toil hard or make others do it. The courage and fortitude they display in any field is monumental. Their inventions or concepts will be used by the world at large for a long time to come. If they are immoral and dishonest, the world comes to know about it quite late and much harm would have been done by then! Even if they are honest and act with integrity, opposition to their policies does crop up (especially in politics or statecraft).

One fine morning, such people suffer due to their own virtues. With a positive force backing the persons' destinies, they overcome hurdles and carve a niche for themselves in the history of their country. With a negative force at work, they are despised and dreaded, sometimes for reasons unknown! Adventure in any field of activity is a way of life for them and their thirst for probing into the unknown is phenomenal. Either waging war or negotiating peace - both are vocations very appealing to the 2 & 9 people. It is a queer stroke of destiny that very few edifices they make survive the onslaught of time. With correct and auspicious Name Numbers and favourable dates for commencing important work, the 2 & 9 personalities shine well in life and become successful.

★ Newsmakers of 2 & 9:

Mahatma Gandhi

Alexei Kosygin

Thomas Clifford Allbutt

Mungo Park

Havelock Ellis

Chandrika Kumaratunga

Walter Chrysler

NAME NUMBERS AND THEIR INTERPRETATIONS

If the sum total of the values of the letters in your name adds up to a 2, then you come under the influence of the Number 2. As days go by, you will slowly feel the effects and characteristics of this number 2. Let us look into the qualities of those having the Name numbers set under this number of Moon:

■ **Name No.11**: Those having 11 as their name number will come up in life by their sheer faith in God. They will profit by various means very easily. They may be riddled with unforeseen problems and dangers, as if their faith is being tested. Sometimes, they tend to meddle with matters that do not concern them. They are likely to be let down by their family and friends. If they have faith in God, they will definitely attain great heights in life. If they lack faith, they are bound to face a lot of setbacks.

■ **Name No.20**: This spiritual number represents a drumbeat heralding triumph or victory. People having this Name number work for liberation and social reforms. They are capable of providing relief to the masses from grief and struggles. The world will admire them. When they work with selfish motives, they are extremely dangerous and highly destructive. Those with name number 20 may excel in medical practice using toxic medicines and dealing with poisonous drugs. They possess the ability to awaken the sleeping masses and lead them to very great achievements. When they go out of their way to satisfy their selfish needs, they are bound to meet with failure or disaster. (Hitler, born on the 20th, spurred Germany into war and faced a humiliating defeat. He is a very good example of this Name number. He was represented by the battle drum that goaded the people to pursue a selfish goal which led to destruction).

■ **Name No.29**: Those under this Name number often find it necessary to go to court to settle disputes. They will experience all sorts of problems in their families and will generally be let down by family and friends. Those who praised them yesterday may curse them today. These people live a life of mental agony and sorrow with their life partner. They get into deep troubles with the opposite sex. Any remedial measures taken to come out of such troubles may result in delayed solutions and huge loss of money and this aggravates the existing problem too. The personal life will be full of ups and downs. Family life consists of events similar to the feats in a circus! Unless the name number is corrected properly, these people will encounter problems forever.

■ Name No.38: The people under this name number will be honest, peace loving and gentle. When it is a name number of a person or a business, it will earn the help of the influential. This Name number can bring great success. People under this number will make rapid development and earn fame and wealth even from very humble beginnings. At times, they will face a lot of dangers and get cheated by bad people, resulting in unforeseen difficulties. **Even their death will be sudden, rather unexpected and unusual.**

■ Name No.47: Those who come up very fast in the life can be seen amongst the people having this name number. They will be very much concerned about their own progress and will work out plans to achieve the same and will not rest until they reach their goal. As for as money matters are concerned, they will be very lucky and can be considered as fortunate people. Many people of this number tend to lose their eyesight at one stage. Even the best available treatment maybe in vain and they suffer very much. It is better for those interested in the habit of hunting to abstain from it and also from flesh-eating.

■ Name No.56: This number is full of wonders. Though this number tends to bring fortune and fame, it is used by those practicing various forms of occultism and divination. This number can free a person from all ties and can break shackles of any kind. Locks would open automatically by their supernatural powers. Even the animals inside the cage would find their way out. As too much of an explanation would not be conducive for a clear thinking, I do not wish to pursue this subject any further. (As explained earlier, the number 29 represents powers of the body and mind, whereas Number 56 gives magical powers). These people will lose their wealth and fame all of a sudden.

■ **Name No. 65:** This number denotes divine grace and progress in spiritual life. It will earn the support of wealthy and powerful patrons. Marital life will be blissful. Persons under this Name number may be sometimes injured in accidents and may have cuts or bruises on their bodies.

■ **Name No. 74:** These people have great affinity towards their religion. They run short of money often. They will introduce social and religious reforms and spread their principles. However, this is not a desirable name number, as it is best suited only for hermits and priests and is not favourable to others. Those who have this name number always remain worried about something or the other.

■ **Name No. 83.** This Name Number bestows prestigious posts which will earn the respect and adoration of many. They will achieve a life of splendor and authority. These people may be considered successful.

■ **Name No.92:** This number signifies gold, silver, land, wealth and possession of yogic power. If people having this Name number can carefully practice the art of yogic breathing, they may even acquire the power of Astral projection.

■ **Name No. 101:** Those under this name number will be helped by governments or by the people of authority rather than by their own efforts. There will be lots of obstacles in their business. Slump in business will be common. This cannot be considered a lucky number.

LOVE AND MARRIAGE

FOR THOSE BORN ON THE 2nd, 11th, 20th AND 29th OF ANY MONTH

Moon is your planet. Just as it waxes and wanes, so are your moods too. Your power of imagination helps you understand the situation you are placed in (or even that of the others whom you are in relation with). But you have some compulsions of your own, which force you to act in a particular way that may not be palatable to your partner in love or marriage.

Your number is 2 and it vibrates favourably to those born on the 7th or its series of dates. With suitable name numbers, your number may vibrate favourably to or attracts those born on the 1st, 4th, 2nd, 3rd, 6th and their series.

Generally, 1,3,4,6 and their series are numbers of your partners that become passive to yours and hence a relationship is possible.

It is advised to "look before you leap" when you try to have a lasting relation with Number 9 people. Their vibes may not agree with yours and a high degree of tolerance or diplomacy may be required. So is the case of Number 8 people with whom it is difficult for the Number 2 persons to live with as husband or wife.

MISCELLANY

The Number 2 people tend to worry constantly and are never satisfied even when others acknowledge their success. Suspicious nature and fickle -mindedness are the negative traits that need to be overcome. The type of upbringing is a very important factor for the children born under Number 2 because Moon gives a "fluid" like mind. It may rush towards any pit or slope in the path of life. But the positive points about their character and performance, if fully exploited, will make the whole world worship them. The pity with the lives of these people is that even when they give judicious advice or counsel, there are no takers. They work rather on a mental plane than physical, although there are good athletes and sportsmen falling in this category. Many, as seen in the history of numerology, take up theatre arts or such other vocations. Their intuitive power (with the right destiny number) or imagination helps them view life from a healthy stand point.

For the people who are ruled by Moon the dates 7, 16 and 25 of every month are lucky. Good gains and benefits are expected on those dates subject to Destiny and Name Numbers. Destiny Number 7 will bring lasting happiness. 25th is luckier than other dates in matters of deriving benefit from others. 1st, 10th, 19th, 28th are also lucky dates. Avoid 2nd, 11th, 20th and 29th for any important work especially involving public and business.

8th, 9th, 18th, 26th, 27th are unfortunate dates to people ruled by Number 2. People born under 7 will render good help.

They must choose light green which is extremely lucky when they wear clothes or paint their premises. Unlucky colours are red, black and dark blue. As for metals, Silver is more favourable. Pearls, Moonstone, or Cat's eye would do well for wearing next to skin.

NUMBERS AND NEWS

"I CHING" -a Chinese system that uses 2 small sticks depicting the duality of life was used by an Eastern astrologer recently to predict that inanimate objects like buildings, monuments and towers looking alike and not connected to each other should not be in close proximity; it may spell danger!

Did he mean the "Twin Towers" of W.T.C. in USA which was incidentally destroyed on the 11th September, 2001? *(Note: -Number 11 also resembles the towers!)*

NUMBER 3 - JUPITER

Jupiter rules those born on the 3rd, 12th, 21st and 30th of any month in a year. People whose Destiny Numbers (Name Numbers also) add up to a 3 also fall under this category. In India, Jupiter is called "GURU" which means "Preceptor" or "Teacher" or "Remover of Darkness".

Jupiter, the largest planet radiating three times as much heat as it receives from the Sun, is also an important one in the solar system. It represents "energy" radiated towards other planets (especially Earth) after absorbing the same from Sun. The Number 3 people signified by this are as such, energetic, hardworking, patriotic, magnanimous, and dutiful. They are ready to sacrifice anything for the cause they espouse, sometimes misplacing their sympathy with the undeserving ones. They have a strong sense of discipline; they readily obey orders and expect others also to do the same. Honesty, fair play, an attitude of service to fellow-humans even at the cost of their own interests are certain sterling qualities they possess. Though they are ambitious and efficient, they do not follow devious means to derive benefit. Self-esteem and honourable conduct are their forte. These are the positive qualities of Number 3 people.

On the other hand, if the negative vibrations dominate the persons born under Number 3, they prove to be over-confident, egoistic, lazy, extravagant and rude. Such people would undo the work of all others in a society or country because of their selfishness or greed for power. No wonder these people achieve power and wealth faster than the ones who are "positively charged" by the cosmic energy! The world looks at them with awe and respect because they reach immeasurable heights under the very nose of their "positive" counterparts. That is what is called destiny!

However, both the lots use their intelligence and oratorical skill in their own style of functioning, though the aims differ! Now, let us discuss about these "Jupiterians" according to their Birth and Destiny Numbers.

What the Birth Dates signify

■ Date - 3   Organising ability, high degree of common sense, oratorical power, intuition, strong desire to achieve the goal and never-say-die attitude towards lives are some of the basic qualities that mark the personality of those born on 3rd of any month. Though there are many scholars who belong to this category, there are people in this lot who do not believe in formal education because their erudition is surprisingly high. They may have a tumultuous past but the way they rise in public life, particularly after their middle age is really an interesting story. Discipline and daring are the watchword in their lives but when they may have to violate the rules which they themselves set, they hardly resent it. They are loyal to the cause they espouse, but are ready to sacrifice anything, if it would help them to acquire fame or money. Hence we may call these people "versatile opportunists" what is puzzling to a natural observer is that those born on the 3rd of any month, one half of them are self-effacing hardworking disciplinarians, but the other half (maybe due to a negative destiny or name number) are good show men. Ironically, both the lots attain fame and command respect in the society. Though they serve the society appreciably, the later half of their career or life become complicated and invites unnecessary problems.

■ Date - 12   If you find someone in the circles of society you live in or visit frequently, who is self-effacing, hard working, loyal to the cause and true to his salt, in all probabilities he could have been born on the 12th of any month. These people who are born on the 12th sacrifice their comforts, wealth and labour to ensure the well-being of those dependent on them or in the larger sense, the society or country in which they live. They have an innate ability to speak on various subjects convincingly, but it is difficult to convince them in any discussion because they need irrefutable proof. Some of them are highly opinionated and when their opinion is proved to be wrong, their lives undergo a drastic change. Their patriotism is infectious and if they are interested in religion, they take it seriously though even in such matters they seek logic and reason. Many who are born on the 12th are viewed by others as lucky, but the fact is otherwise. They deserve whatever best in life because after toiling hard in the fields and sowing the seeds, they certainly deserve the benefit. Their versatility and service to the world is remembered for a long time to come even after their death. A difficult or penurious childhood is common in the lives of this lot, but when those born on other dates crumble and fall prey to the circumstances, those born on 12th view the challenges philosophically and conquer them. Though the mankind is amply benefited by the services of these people, there is also a sordid side of nature in some of them which sometimes turns their admirers into critics or even enemies. However, their assumed mission is never fully accomplished and towards the end of their lives they would feel that something "more" could have been done for the cause they espoused all their life. This date of birth is one of the dates that evoke interest due to the fact that those born on this date, however good they may be, find themselves at loggerheads with their conscience at one time or the other in life. To right a wrong, they may have to do something that is wrong. The world may call it by any parlance, but it is either the act of god or the act of destiny!

■ Date - 21   Experienced numerologists generally believe that of all the four dates of birth under Number 3, 21 is the strongest date. The reason may be that they are more practical in life and their actions are result-oriented. The very prominent quality of intelligence or commonsense attributed to the Jupiterian dates of birth has an interesting twist in the case of those born on the 21st. Whichever profession they are placed in, they don't give room for sentiments or public interest in their methodology and forge ahead, come what may. Judging their actions by the trials and tribulations they overcome, one will be forced to conclude that any high-handedness or extreme steps taken by them were not just for serving their own ends alone but here is a "common" purpose too! At times, they take abnormal risks either in their career or in their personal lives and luck may not be on their side!

■ **Date - 30**   The persons born on the 30th have a queer side to their personality. They always use whatever resources they have at hand to arrive at a solution. Exploring countries or minds or the intricacies of art and science or even modern weaponry, becomes their favourite interest. They would not mind the obstacles and follow only the command of their own minds, be it right or wrong! They have novel ideals in pursuing their goal, but very few can excel them in execution of their plans. Versatility and single-minded devotion are the hallmark of their character and their impact on the society, art, theatre and politics is a longlasting phenomenon. If their purpose of action is noble, sky is the limit for their achievements. On the other hand, if they indulge in anti-social activities they do achieve some success initially, but soon they will be ruined beyond apprehension.

People born under Birth Number 3 (born on the 3rd,12th, 21st and 30th of any month) and with various Destiny Numbers will find their lives as follows:

BIRTH NUMBER 3 & DESTINY NUMBER 1 (JUPITER -SUN)

Both Jupiter and Sun are mutual friends and as far as the career and general prospects are concerned they are "supposed" to be lucky (Not in all aspects!). Honesty, hard work and discipline which are the common factors of both 3 and 1 are very supportive of all the plans of these people and ensure success. Professions involving medicine, chemicals and statecraft prove to be both successful and soul-satisfying. But, media, cinema, music and the like, though offering good opportunities, do not give satisfaction. They cause a lot of anxieties and drive these natives mad for unknown reasons. What more, their personal lives are adversely affected. Though the people of 3 & 1 group are good managers, born leaders and able administrators, due to unavoidable circumstances they wind up one course of their lives and venture into another. But wherever they are placed, they render unforgettable service to mankind and the posterity does not forget them. In politics, with the right support of Name Numbers and with favourable dates of commencing any important work, these people become indispensable and reach the top but face opposition or quit the post voluntarily. Artistes and writers find the going difficult at times and indulge themselves in unusual methods to solve their problems. Hence, they must exercise caution!

⭐ Newsmakers of 3 & 1:

Alfred Nobel

Tom Cruise

Tiger Woods

George Eastman

Florence Nightingale

Henry Ford

BIRTH NUMBER 3 & DESTINY NUMBER 2 (JUPITER - MOON)

The ambitious, dignified, philosophical and disciplined 3 in partnership with Destiny Number 2 who is friendly, imaginative and sympathetic represents a good blend. These 3 & 2 people are specialists in managing finance, investments and trusts of charitable nature. Their social consciousness, love for animals and plants, versatility and glib of the tongue come handy, while organising people for a business or a political struggle or sometimes, even a spiritual pursuit. Lethargy and the habit of postponing matters of vital importance are enemies of this combination. They may not be very happy souls in marriage or love and in most cases they only are to blame. But, they never exhibit their inner feelings. Their success in public life depends upon lucky Name Numbers and choice of favourable dates for any important political activity. They find that all their dreams and ambitions -barring a few, are not fulfilled, although they have toiled hard. They are advised to remedy the shortcomings by Numerology.

★ Newsmakers of 3 & 2:

Salim Ali (Ornithologist)
Mother of Auroville -Mirra Alfassa
Sir Philip Sidney
King George V
Raja Chelliah
Cecil B.DeMille

BIRTH NUMBER 3 & DESTINY NUMBER 3
(JUPITER - JUPITER)

The combination of 3 & 3 in any person gives him more courage, a greater versatility, outspokenness, sacrificial tendency and lasting friendships. At the same time, this increases the impulsiveness, headstrong attitude and restlessness. But the people who are signified by this number combination work without any grudge or grouse. The honesty of purpose, doggedness and single-minded devotion to duty will help them overcome very serious problems in life and achieve their goals. They have a researching nature which helps them invent or discover things that are meant for ameliorating the problems of the mankind. However big they may be in the society, they always think and act in favour of the down-trodden and the oppressed. When they are in the media business they point out boldly the flaws in the administration and the vagaries of human life. Sometimes they see themselves in a different land or in a different atmosphere, re-starting their lives afresh. Either they are bigots or liberals fighting for freedom. The successful always claim that God gave them everything. The suffering types bear with the agony smilingly. That answers all questions about this category!

★ Newsmakers of 3 & 3:
Andrei Sakharov
Anne Frank
Asa Griggs Candler
Amartya Sen
Alistair MacLean
Shirin Ebadi

NUMBER 3 - JUPTIER
BIRTH NUMBER 3 & DESTINY NUMBER 4
(JUPITER - URANUS)

Viewing from the stand point of Number 3 (Jupiter), Number 4(Uranus) does not confer positive vibrations in certain fields of activity. When 3 is the Birth Number denoting ambitious nature (making purposeful efforts in life), power of oratory and the spirit of doing something worthwhile for the mankind. Number 4 which makes the natives practical, down-to-earth, freedom-loving, calculative and always innovating, does a lot to the combination, strengthening the alliance. But that is not all! The peculiar secretive nature of Uranus which goes "out of tune" with Jupiter on some specific occasions, "eclipses" the fortune of the latter. Misunderstandings arise both in the office and at home and unless handled promptly, they take an ugly shape. In their own spheres of life, this combination of 3 & 4 gives good status, spiritual strength, popularity, reward for hard work and support from Government. There is one peculiarity with the events of their lives. On occasions when the planetary influence (positive) goes weak, these natives get involved in problems related to opposite sex. Many either avoid marriage or find their wives or girlfriends disappear from the earth; some of them even face law suits! This, however, in no way affects the prospects of Number 3 & 4 natives much, although the events of such nature remain as indelible scars in their hearts. Sometimes they are considered "cruel" or heartless, though the natives could justify their actions on grounds of "saving the head by losing the hat"! But destiny acts through people of such combination only to re-write history. Several of the people under this category brave odds to establish what they consider justice, mostly in the interest of their community, nation or the world in the larger sense. It is a mystery that having achieved their purpose, they "feel satisfied" (may be they think that their innings are over!) and lead a solitary life thereafter. Their inborn quality of viewing life from an unusual angle is phenomenal and with positive vibrations of Jupiter rather manifested, they become immaculate souls on this earth!

★ Newsmakers of 3 & 4:

Mike Tyson

Frank Sinatra

Cesar Pelli

William Crawford Gorgas

David H.koch

Arnold Schwarzenegger

BIRTH NUMBER 3 & DESTINY NUMBER 5
(JUPITER - MERCURY)

If Fate brings two people with two different attitudes in life together, Freewill makes the company survive and flourish. This can be explained by the lives of people born under Birth Number 3 -Destiny Number 5 combination. When 3 gives versatility, discipline, devotion towards duty and dynamism, 5 gives the same person popularity, quick-to-decide nature (which may be mistaken for gambling nature at times) intuition, foresight in business, abnormal activity, flexible character and magnetism. This mixture of qualities, even without any "providential" help makes the person of 3 & 5 to decide his own course of action in any predicament. Unlike most of the other persons, this 3 & 5 person leaves an indelible impression on the society in which he lives. Even the hasty actions of persons born under this numerical alliance prove to be successful because of the intuition they possess. In business ventures of any nature, they shine. If they do not own any, at least they give their valuable advice. In businesses related to theatre, silver screen or press, their services or performance will be remembered for a long time to come (The reason may be that most of them easily understand at the first instant the character of the persons they meet). Some of them do not mind to follow "devious" means to achieve their ends. These people seldom "retire" from active life. They pursue one activity or the other until their physical conditions do not permit any further. People of this combination are innovative, artistic, always conscious of what is to be done, judicious in money matters (miserly, if negative vibrations dominate) and follow a "think big - act big" policy in their business. Unfavourable "swings" of Numbers in their lives make them reckless gamblers, but the way they face losses and challenges is legendary! It is a pity that these personalities "overdo" their bit and suffer, although they rebound very fast. They have an innate cleverness in keeping their affairs secret. It includes their love affairs or secrets of national interest also. They present themselves to the world outside as a contended lot, but brood within that their talents or performances have gone unrecognised. No doubt, when they die they wish to be born again to complete the work! Many of the 3 & 5 people should learn how to tackle the problems related to their spouse or children.

★ Newsmakers of 3 & 5:

Abraham Lincoln

Marlon Brando

F.D. Roosevelt

Olof Palme

Antony Quinn

Ben Johnson

BIRTH NUMBER 3 & DESTINY NUMBER 6
(JUPITER - VENUS)

This is generally believed in astrological circles that a person born with the conjunction of Jupiter and Venus has conflicting qualities. If both the planets are of positive vibrations manifesting their powers on the natives of 3 & 6, lucky and favourable results are conferred on them. If otherwise, negative or mixed results are seen. Such other combination of any two numbers may not produce as bad results as these. When discipline and honesty of purpose play an important role in the life of a 3 person with a Destiny Number 6, the artistic, ever-enthusiastic and resourceful nature of 6 gives a boost to all the noble efforts. Thus, the person becomes immortalised in the hearts of mankind. However, there is always some kind of deficiency in his or her personal life (when the 3 & 6 person broods over it and suffers the 6 & 3 tries to forget it!). People born under this combination find themselves elated during their period of glory or popularity and forget that one day the same people who praised and adored them may take cudgels in their hands and oppose! Of course, those who know the quirk of human fate thoroughly (the philosophic types) are very much balanced in their outlook and would carry on with their service to the community in which they live. Such people -even if they are in politics which makes people crave for power -succeed in their efforts, unmindful of the opposition or reverses they face. Their policy is, "If you can't strike the way it must go, strike the way it goes!"

As writers or artists who depict the world they live in, they choose the subjects like metaphysics, spiritualism, crime detection, sex or witchcraft. Their aim is to give a message to the public, a message hitherto unknown. That's all!

★ Newsmakers of 3 & 6:

Clement Attlee

Stanley Baldwin

Boris Spassky

Warren Buffet

Pablo Neruda

BIRTH NUMBER 3 & DESTINY NUMBER 7
(JUPITER - NEPTUNE)

These 3 & 7 people who have both Jupiter and Neptune as their governing planets shoot into fame and popularity easily. But they are unable to continue enjoying the fruits of their positions for a long time.

NUMBER 3 - JUPTIER

At least those who retain their status suddenly face some reverses to their position at some stage. The practical disciplinarian with a spiritual or super conscious mind - as per rule, should deserve more. But the unfavourable numerical conjunction of Numbers 3 and 7 causes error of judgement on vital issues or at crucial moments and creates an atmosphere of opposition or enmity. Since the governing planets are related to pursuits employing brain and mind powers, their natives of this combination are widely found in the professions connected to performing arts or silver screen though teaching, consultancy, science or politics attract them. In politics, they do reach a covetable position but often suffer a jolt from which they find it very difficult to recover. They have many "firsts" to their credit - be it any field, but the glory does not last long for reasons of "cosmological mystery." When they ascend to power, they forget conveniently the harsh reality of the fact that they may have to descend from their pedestal one day. Though Neptune is a planet of spirituality or Wisdom and as a rule should confer wise counsel at the right moment, the forces of destiny make these people ignore the timely warning. Those who understand the course of their destiny and heed the advice, shine very well. They have permanent fortunes and acquire wealth and fame, if they choose lucky names and lucky dates for functioning. This point is more relevant in the professions connected to Jupiter (Mars also is conducive, sometimes) such as, Banking, law, military, religion and in many cases sports and arts also.

★ Newsmakers of 3 & 7:

Queen Elizabeth II

Sir Anthony Eden

Sir Winston Churchill

Ramsay Macdonald

George Bush (Senior)

Mel Gibson

BIRTH NUMBER 3 & DESTINY NUMBER 8 (JUPITER - SATURN)

As Jupiter and Saturn are neither inimical nor friendly, the vibrations of Numbers 3 and 8 also remain balanced in the lives of these people. However, the general tendency of 8 is to retard, reflect and render retributive justice. Unless the people born on the dates of 3 "watch their steps," they may fall into "abyss!" The over -ambitious (sometimes, greedy...) and reckless or gambling attitude of Jupiterians may be checked by the philosophic or suspicious -natured Saturn and the results are somewhat balanced. This combination is of strange nature, because the pushy, boastful, demonstrative and fast performing Number 3, if not strong enough or dominant, will allow itself to be influenced by the conservative, undemonstrative, slow and secretive Number 8. You may imagine where this combination stands (especially, in their married life!)

On acquiring positive vibrations by choosing correct Name numbers and auspicious dates for action, the great qualities of this 3 & 8 type surface. They are self-effacing, hardworking and ambitious to prove their point despite odds and are humanitarian in nature. While under many other combinations you may find too many important and popular personalities, 3 & 8 has comparatively less number of people as such. But, their contribution to any sphere they live in is too great to explain.

Some important personalities born under 3 & 8 serries.

★ Newsmakers of 3 & 8:

Alexander Graham Bell

Rudyard Kipling

Martha Stewart

Sun Yat - Sen

Father Damien

Rupert Brooke

NUMBER 3 - JUPTIER

BIRTH NUMBER 3 & DESTINY NUMBER 9
(JUPITER - MARS)

Jupiter and Mars are mutual "friends" in astrology. The numbers which mystically represent these two planets in the same order are 3 & 9 who are also friendly and make a good team causing positive vibrations. When due to the quirk of fate, the Name numbers or dates of important assignments go wrong, negative results occur.

Courageous, quick in action, prudently religious, enterprising, scheming against the adversary, strong in likes or dislikes, forceful and enthusiastic are the persons born under 3 & 9 combination. Their doggedness and spirit of resistance to the odds of life are legendary. When they are educated they rise to high posts in government, especially in politics. In manufacturing machines of daily use they are innovative and take any risks in ensuring success of the project. Their vigour and dash are very appealing even in the media business or in histrionic activities. They convince others by hook or crook. They can speak convincingly or coercively depending upon situations. As such, if the field of their activities demands that they have to assert themselves, they do it forcefully and sometimes even their advisors or sub-ordinates happen to protest. They can create and at the same time destroy also! Sometimes, people who observe them think that these 3 & 9 types are "dangerous." Of course, if not on all occasions, on some occasions it is true!. But, actually they are opportunistic and they root out opposition either physically or using their mental strength. Mars is the lord of wars and militancy and when its vibrations are strong in a person, it is better to keep a safe distance from him or her! In any field they are placed in, their role is an important factor to ensure execution of plans. This makes others think that the 3 & 9 types are revolutionaries. In fact, all of them are not!

When the positive types consist of diplomats, able military leaders, lawyers, charismatic politicians and artistes or performers of mass appeal, the negative ones have their own list of quarrelsome charlatans, opportunists, aggressive characters and sometimes even people who kill themselves. (This is because of living in extreme ends of emotion which, if avoided, will confer good results). Positive or Negative - they are good planners and also doers. It is only this lot that changes the face of this world off and on.

★ **Newsmakers of 3 & 9:**

Air Marshal Gerald Ernest Gibbs

Benazir Bhutto

Connie Francis

Amrita Sher-Gil

K.N.Rao

Vladimir K. Zworykin

NAME NUMBERS AND THEIR INTERPRETATIONS

If the sum total of the values of the letters in the name adds up to 3, this number will influence you. If the birth date or the destiny number is 3, then the name number could also be under 3. If those born on different dates have their Name numbers under 3, they will lead dissatisfied lives. That is to say that they will work hard, slog all their lives and others will enjoy the fruits of their hard work!

■ **Name No.3:** This name number denotes hard work, intelligence, success and a comfortable life. They will be highly educated and will gradually progress in life.

■ **Name No. 12:** These people naturally possess the ability to attract people by their power of speech. They sacrifice their lives for the welfare and happiness of others by shouldering their burdens too.

NUMBER 3 - JUPTIER

■ **Name No. 21:** These people are self-centered and concerned about their own happiness and matters profitable to them. With great determination, they rise steadily in life and reach the pinnacle of success. Their tactful behaviour helps them to solve all their problems. They struggle hard in their early days but achieve success and happiness as they grow up. They will attain and retain good positions permanently in their lives.

■ **Name No. 30:** These people tend to live in a world of fantasy. They are wise thinkers. They like to do what they feel is right. At times, just for their own satisfaction they get involved in certain difficult tasks, without expecting any returns. They have less interest in making money. They know their minds and conquer the same easily. They gain mystic powers through mind control and related mental exercises.

■ **Name No. 39:** These people are very sincere and hardworking. Invariably, the name and fame that are rightfully due to them will be enjoyed by others. They work unceasingly for the welfare of others. They are not as healthy as the other Number 3 people at some stage of their life and are prone to some kind of skin diseases.

■ **Name No. 48:** They will be more interested in religious matters, but face opposition in matters that involve the society at large. They will do a lot of work for public welfare, and create problems for themselves while attempting to do things beyond their capacity. Fate is against them most of the time.

■ **Name No. 57:** This number gives victory or success in the beginning, but brings about gradual downfall and loss of interest in the end. Life which progresses at a very swift pace will grind to a halt all of a sudden. People named under this number will achieve great heights from humble beginnings but will later revert to their original positions.

63

■ **Name No. 66:** This number denotes dynamism and oratorical skills, perfection in the fine arts, patronage from the government authorities and also a comfortable life.

■ **Name No. 75:** All of a sudden they attain great fame. They will make good friends very soon. Unexpectedly, they become very popular. Fame and comforts will come in search of them. They become good poets and writers.

■ **Name No. 84:** Early days will be full of struggles and worries. They earn enemies unnecessarily. Travelling benefits them. They do not get rewards commensurate to their efforts. They improve themselves to some extent spiritually. Though generally lacking in enthusiasm at first, they can go to extremes, if need be! If the influence of their birth date is favourable, they can be great achievers.

■ **Name No. 93:** These people are capable of doing marvellous things. They improve their worldly knowledge and are lucky to have their desires fulfilled. They excel in the field of histrionics through which they attain more fame. They earn through many business pursuits and lead very dignified lives.

■ **Name No. 102:** This number signifies success at first, followed by struggles and confusion. These people cannot be called lucky.

LOVE AND MARRIAGE

FOR THOSE BORN ON THE 3ʳᵈ, 12ᵗʰ, 21ˢᵗ AND 30ᵗʰ OF ANY MONTH

Jupiter is your planet. Just as its gigantic size in the sky, you have a large and accommodative heart which may be bursting with kindness. And it may be the cause of others (especially, your ladylove or spouse!) taking undue advantage also; you have the knack of making your marriage survive or successful, due to a high degree of common sense (a Jupiterian quality!) or your capacity to foresee the future.

NUMBER 3 - JUPTIER

Your number is 3 which is considered "sacred" by Pythagoras. Celtic scriptures speak very high of this number. You have a natural vibration and attraction towards those born on the 3rd, 5th and 9th and their series, suggesting a happy love life or married life.

The numbers 6 and 8 and their series are to be avoided for long term relationships as they imply a great deal of tension for you both domestically and professionally.

With those born on the 1st, 2nd, 4th and 7th and their series of dates you will sail along without any hiccups, though the first-said three numbers are the most harmonious lot.

MISCELLANY

The governing planet Jupiter, basically a benefic, makes any person of any Destiny number a versatile person with a purpose to live. Mostly it radiates positive vibrations which remedy the defects of the Destiny number also. If the Destiny number also is a 3, then the Name number only is to be observed or taken care of.

The lucky dates for these Jupiterians are 3rd, 9th, 12th, 18th, 21st, 27th and 30th of all months. Dates making a 6, (like 6th, 15th and 24th) are not favourable and are considered unlucky. Even such dates making a 6 as Destiny number are to be avoided.

Persons of numbers 2, 3 and 1 will be helpful to the Number 3 people. No tangible help of permanent or temporary nature from Numbers 6, 8 (and sometimes 5 also) will be available. If Destiny number of Number 1, 4 and 5 people is 3, then help can be expected from such people.

Orange, Pink or Mauve is a lucky colour. Amethyst is the lucky stone. Avoid dark blue, green and black.

65

NUMBERS AND NEWS

One of the tools of FENG - SHUI - the Chinese "Vasthu", is a THREE LEGGED FROG! It is considered to be the luck-bringer. Symbolically, it is said to represent the 3 dimensions of the physical world or the Triplicity of the earthly life - creation, preservation, annihilation (The fourth leg is the invisible TIME).

NUMBER 4 - URANUS

Represented by Number 4, Uranus, the seventh planet from the sun, is an eccentrically banded giant, more than four times the size of Earth. Though Sir William Herschel is officially said to have discovered Uranus in 1781, John Flamstead, Astronomer Royal of England who built Greenwich observatory was the actual discoverer in the year 1690 itself. Flamstead was not just an astronomer but a well-known Astrologer too! Interestingly, the basic character of Uranus, as described in Astrological sciences, that is to say, affecting the life and career of humans, especially people in public life or celebrities, eclipsed Flamstead's discovery also! Such is the mysterious and unexpected way Uranus acts!

Uranus takes about seven years orbiting each sign of Zodiac and together with Neptune decides the mundane affairs on this earth affecting politics, science, religion and natural resources in general, and also super natural abilities in specific. Both are said to be "Karmic" in nature in the sense, their cosmological vibrations affect the life on the earth in a way that the cause and effect seem to be the unpredictable!

Uranus is malefic, sometimes more malefic than Saturn or Mars. Revolution, unexpected changes in life, disease, natural calamities, violent changes in the countries, unusual behaviour, evil desires, communal or racial unrest - are attributed to the unfavourable zodiacal journey of Uranus. Though a policeman or a criminal - both follow the cult of violence in the literal sense, we know that the former saves our lives but the latter does not. Thus, a Uranus person could be a cop, or a criminal! If we analyse the positive "swing" of Uranus' vibrations on us, we understand from the ancient texts that Uranus bestows many good things for a happy mundane life. Understanding the mysteries of life, skills of writing (on subjects like occultism, crime detection etc.,) espionage, mathematics, military strategies, poetry, religion, adventures and metaphysics are subjects in which they easily shine. They are revolutionaries in their own way and we can find more number of people under Number 4 category who "cause" a war or a revolution than those who are actually involved in it. Their style of functioning is peculiar or unique, whichever field they are placed in. They have sudden changes in their lives - so sudden that they themselves may not foresee it. Though they look egotistic, selfish or rude outwardly, their healing touch to the suffering humanity is known only to those who closely watch them or understand them. Those who are selfish or greedy do get money or wealth but squander it sooner or later. But those who are philanthropic and god-fearing, though called "misers" at times, are great souls who provide permanent help to the needy. They only want to ensure that their sympathy remains with those who deserve it.

With benign Destiny numbers and Name Numbers adding to the positive vibrations of this Birth Number, these Number 4 people may become icons to the posterity. Now let us study the lives of people with Birth Number 4 (born on the 4lh, 13th, 22nd and 31st any month) and with various Destiny numbers.

What the Birth Dates signify

■ Date - 4   The birth dates do not categorically suggest a particular profession to those born on any specific date due to the fact that interaction among nations and free exchange of ideas have already revolutionised the concept of free trade and employment. But, the birth

NUMBER 4 - URANUS

dates under the enigmatic planet Uranus suggest one thing in common about these people. Revolution or renaissance marks Uranus and those born on the 4th prove it. They are found in all walks of life, -politics, religion, business, scientific research or mathematics, military or literature and music. They are basically bold and brave and strive hard to innovate and improve the system of which they are a part. Like all other number 4 people (born on the 13th, 22nd and 31st of any month), they have an insatiable desire to research into any subject they handle and experiment with the results they arrive at. Unlike the number 3 people, the service of this lot to the mankind catches the immediate attention of the world in most cases. Extreme sports or histrionics both offer vocations to them. Success comes to them only when they do not express their anger and offend others. If they succumb to the temptation of exhibiting their emotions or bad temper, they may miss golden opportunities to promote their own interest.

■ Date – 13   These persons are bold and forthright. In nation-building, industrial enterprises, religion and politics their opinions cause a flutter. Unexpected changes, positive or negative, are bound to happen in their lives. Destiny leads them to such situations that they may have to take sides in any dispute, even if they do want to stay neutral. In some not-much-known fields, they would venture and surprisingly become successful. A few of them even become heads of such organisations. But in any walk of life they involve themselves, they become trendsetters and enjoy lasting fame, until somebody who was close to them causes a problem. In some cases it could be someone from the opposite sex. They hold some vital information about their own trade or about other people's activities. Sometimes, they espouse a wrong cause or support wrong persons, but are quick to dump them, if need be. Some people of this category use their charms to their advantage and become comparatively more successful than others born on Number 4 dates. At times, their actions prove to be puzzling and present an interesting study.

69

MY FORTUNE

■ **Date – 22**   Either path-breaking inventions or hair-splitting intrigues, those who are born on the 22nd are very capable of doing. There are umpteen number of people under this category who have contributed to the improvement of lives of their countrymen and added value to their country's economy. At the same time, those with negative vibrations have wrought havoc on the society. one thing is certain –good or bad, they are efficient strategists and their power of speech and concerted action come handy in what they choose to do. They have an in-born ability to calculate the profit and loss even before they indulge in any business (it is interesting to note that a good number of prodigious mathematicians, professional soldiers and bravest revolutionaries are born on 22nd!). There is no job or business these people cannot do and almost all of them easily win acclaim and success in their chosen profession. If as businessmen their activities transcend geographical borders, as religious personalities or teachers of morals they fathom the murky depths of human minds. (When we discuss in general, the personalities born on various birth dates, we will be certainly surprised to note that the date 22nd has myriad characters, from both the extremes! For example, Robert Oppenheimer was instrumental in designing atom bombs dropped on Japan, but on observing the destruction it caused, he became the most vociferous protester of nuclear weapons. He was born on 22nd April).

■ **Date – 31** Though a few of those born on this date choose the subtle professions like fine arts, cinema etc., a good number of people tend to become politicians and administrators. Interestingly, they rise to top positions using not only their innate skill of judging people and situations but also their ability to persuade or even coerce. As rulers of states or administrators or even as military leaders, they exhibit a rare sense of purpose and dutifulness. Disappointments do not deter them from doing their duty or discourage them. What is intriguing to a neutral observer of their life is that at any one stage during their life time, their own compatriots may ditch them or part ways. In sports, literature or occultism they innovate and attain stunning success. With favourable destiny and name numbers, they become so famous and successful that posterity would wonder if these people had been doing things using their intuitive ability or with the help of some divine powers. Yet there are occasions in their lifetime that cause concern and anxiety when their plans do not succeed fully. (The negative types under this number are also successful,- at least temporarily, only to ruin the world first and ruin themselves later). Unexpected turns in their lives are common, but they have the ability to conceal their emotions and forge ahead, though not always. The one important lesson the world learns from the lives of the persons born on the 31st day of any month is that they leave a legacy which must be followed and improved for the benefit of mankind.

People born under Birth Number 4 (4th,13th, 22nd and 31st of any month) and with various Destiny Number will find their lives as follows:

BIRTH NUMBER 4 & DESTINY NUMBER 1 (URANUS -SUN)

People born under the dates totalling to the single Number 4 and Destiny Number 1 belong to Uranus - Sun combination. Uranus and Sun are not friendly to each other - astrologically speaking. But, numerologically, No. 4 derives maximum benefit from No.1 in certain walks of life. Both are down-to-earth, practical, domineering and hardworking people. Society, community, religion, politics or statecraft, - be it any field, there these people bring about reforms! When 4 & 1 combination comes under positive vibrations, they shine in politics. They set a personal example of themselves. They unify people and chastise their followers. They encourage those who are honest and bring to book those who are corrupt. Their power of speech is others' envy. They shine as writers but earn the wrath of wrong-doers in the society. As said earlier, the Destiny Number 1 makes the people with Number 4 as Birth Number, lucky. The qualities of Number 4 such as, indecisiveness, using the talents for unclear ends, wasting efforts even on unimportant matters, neglecting one's own health while advising others to be healthy, and in some cases temperamental instability, will bring some peculiar experiences. This is compensated by Number 1 whose merits we have already discussed. Thus, 4 & 1 combination makes a person to rethink or introspect and take a

71

decision in any issue. Interestingly, when the vibrations of Number 1 are of positive nature, the natives of 4 & 1 combination make history and become idols of worship. If negative vibrations dominate - STILL THEY MAKE HISTORY, but in an unconventional way! If a community or a country has to benefit from the deeds of a Number 4 & 1 person, then it is imperative that he has his lucky Name Number under 1 and he should choose for important missions dates such as 1st, 10th, 19th and 28th (28th of any month, though harmonious, will not confer lasting benefit). The power of imagination or speech becomes their forte.

★ Newsmakers of 4 & 1:

George Washington

Maria Montessori

David Blaine

John Logie Baird

Munshi Premchand

Rene Descartes

BIRTH NUMBER 4 & DESTINY NUMBER 2
(URANUS -MOON)

Uranus rules Number 4. Moon rules Number 2.. When the positive vibrations are at the lowest ebb, they suffer more than others due to this unfavourable combination. But when they are at the favourable peak, they keep on climbing the ladder of fame. So may be with any other combination. But this particular one of Number 4 pairing with Number 2 with harmonious Name Numbers and harmonious dates either by Nature or by the choice of the native confers the best possible results. This may be called a numerological coincidence in the lives of people who are born under Numbers 4 and 2 and they are found successful!

Uranus who causes revolution and who is related to mysticism, poesy and uncommon interests, while interacting with the planet Moon (astronomically moon is a satellite of the earth!) which symbolises mind has a good many stories to tell! It produces revolutionary thinkers or unconventional industrialists or performing artistes who follow their own style. The peculiar behaviour of this combination is that **these people do succeed but they have to defeat their counterparts hands down first, -in some way, conventional or otherwise!** They win recognition or awards and they also institute some. From whatever angle you view them, they seem to be "queer" personalities but the mental strength and the drive to achieve that are hidden within, are generally **not** visible to the outside world. The world takes a long time to understand them!

⭐ **Newsmakers of 4 & 2:**
   Barack Obama
   Ramon Magsaysay
   Hosni Mubarak
   Orlando Bloom
   Charlton Heston
   Antoine Christophe Merlin

BIRTH NUMBER 4 & DESTINY NUMBER 3 (URANUS - JUPITER)

Freedom-loving, self-centered, stubborn, suspicious and sometimes eccentric -the Number 4 persons will find a good guide in Number 3, because Number 3 will make them analytical, discerning, introspective, and disciplined. Thus, the basically controversial combination can yield better results in practical life. When others rebound from worries and anxieties very fast or go to extremes of what they think remedies, this 4 & 3 people try to approach the day-to-day problems in a philosophical manner. It is immaterial whether they waste their time, energy or money. The end result only can satisfy them (or dissatisfy them!). The positive lot (probably, with good Name Numbers or efforts taken on chosen days) shine in any field they embark upon. They are self-inspired or self-made. But they do not tolerate those who do not contribute their mite to the society or field of activity. Sometimes, they condemn such people openly and earn their hatred. They operate secretly and cause annoyance or harm even to their friends. When they are aesthetically stung, their "negative" qualities do not harm the people around them. In such cases, they may even become celebrities by using their skills!

They may earn well while under vibrations that guide them to success, but also spend well if they are convinced that their money is used for a purpose that enhances their prestige. In businesses connected to the mind and its powers (but using an unusual skill or style) they excel all others. You may find such successful people in the theater, casinos and even in religious activities or rebellious movements. If the skilled people of this category do not "save for the rainy day", they end up in poverty or servitude. Mostly they speak a lot but perform only on select issues. But when they write or command others to do some work, perfection becomes their watchword!

★ Newsmakers of 4 & 3:

Audrey Hepburn

Fidel Castro

Li Ka-Shing

Alfred Hitchcock

Sri Sri Ravi Shankar (Spiritual teacher)

W.B. Yeats (Author, Nobel Laureate)

BIRTH NUMBER 4 & DESTINY NUMBER 4 (URANUS- URANUS)

This combination is a very interesting one, since the persons born under Uranus-Uranus relationship have given more to the humankind than most of the other combinations. Just as the water tank that provides water to the people in the community but gets drained by itself, the 4 & 4 people serve the society in which they live. In many cases, they forget that the sunshine of their own lives gets "eclipsed" one day. But they have an unusually philosophic mind which gives them the power of viewing life from a healthy standpoint. The positive types serve the humanity more and

74

more and the negative types serve their own ends more and more. Both need an advice: **"Never choose extreme positions!"**

Most of the people born under this category are recognised by their hardworking nature. They never keep their minds free from "plans" or "projects". Anything for the good of the earth (That's their planet too!) and the earthlings keep their minds pre-occupied. Lands, rivers, minerals or chemicals, Logic and Science, politics and military are a few venues in which they operate. As a contrast, a few of them also excel in music and theatre, depending upon the Name Numbers and Zodiacal signs or their dates of original ventures, (it is possible that the earth is surrounded by atmospheric ether and ether is represented by Mercury which plays its role).

The 4 people in general and the 4 & 4 in particular, are rather remembered after their death than during their lifetime. This may be due to the Uranus & Uranus combination or due to the harsh reality that the world recognises its great children always a little late! However, these people who become celebrities are sometimes at loggerheads with destiny! Either their private lives or their near and dear ones suffer in one way or the other. It may be due to the fact that having been engrossed in their worldly duties they forget to pay regular attention to their family. This is a peculiarity with Uranus in general, because he diminishes even the power of Sun and the Moon! But, all the same, there are ups and downs on any road and the 4 & 4 types know better about what ails their journey. The negatively charged 4 & 4 type persons who are typically under the influence of a malefic Uranus are too dangerous to describe.

★ Newsmakers of **4 & 4**:

P.B.Shelley

Michael Faraday

Margaret Thatcher

S.Ramanujan (Prodigious Indian Mathematician)

Clint Eastwood (Hollywood Hero)

J.Robert Oppenheimer (U.S. Scientist of Atom bomb Fame)

Sarah Bernhardt (Singer)

BIRTH NUMBER 4 & DESTINY NUMBER 5
(URANUS - MERCURY)

We generally believe that illusion (Maya in oriental scriptures), an abstract product of the Soul and the Mind, makes the people "blind" to the harsh realities of the world. Illusion is the by-product of emotions in the practical sense and the persons born under Number 4 understand this, utilize this and benefit from this belief system. When Mercury, the fast-moving planet which confers intelligence, dynamism and scholastic excellence, is in conjunction with Uranus in a person's natal chart, the result is wonderful. .Hence the 4 & 5 people know what they want for themselves and also what the world wants from them.

As writers, they give a message that nobody else (under any other combination) would even imagine to give. As politicians or statesmen, they know the knack of staying in power and in the news. As administrators, they have an innate skill of imagining the results of the policies even before they become the law! The Number 4 & 5 combination gives the power of probing the mysteries of human mind, space, soul and metaphysical phenomena. Let these people be in any walk of life, they investigate, innovate and illuminate. In most of the cases, Mercury, represented by Number 5, the "torch - bearer" of the numerological realm, overpowers Uranus. This is possible only when positive vibrations are strong. If negative vibrations emanate from the two planets, the world can no longer survive, because this combination can cause chaos in the cosmos. Surprisingly, Uranus which subjects us to Cause and Effect is acquiescent and so it's basically negative vibrations are held under control by Mercury represented by Number 5!

However, those born under the birth dates totalling to a 4 and Destiny Number 5 are advised to select numbers and dates making a 5, because 4 gives unusual events, revolutionary ideas and unexpected behaviour to a "thinking man". But 5 is not ideal for marital bliss, though Name numbers or Destiny numbers could modify any ill effects. It is better that Number 1 which is a luck-bringer, be widely used.

NUMBER 4 - URANUS

★ Newsmakers of 4 & 5:

Louis Braille

Sir Arthur Conan Doyle

James Coburn

Thomas Jefferson

Floyd Patterson

J.K.Rowling

BIRTH NUMBER 4 & DESTINY NUMBER 6 (URANUS - VENUS)

Revolutionary and also magnetic, scholastic but ignorant of needs of the hour, artistically rebellious, irreligious yet intellectually superior, violent but self-effacing, non-partisan still fulfilling everyone's ambitions, spiritual and society-conscious as well, traditional in thinking but practically modern, ... these are the "first impressions" created in one's mind when he meets a person under 4 & 6 category.! As in the case of conjunctions with positive Numbers, in this particular case also Number 4 people get amply benefited by Destiny Number 6.

When the circumstances are fine, the Birth Number 4 and Destiny Number 6 do not clash with each other's vibrations. Those born under this combination are successful and the usually disharmonious domestic life of Number 4 will become harmonious due to the positive vibrations of 6. But still their married life undergoes turbulent changes. Some even tend to become renouncers! Some others try to find solace in more than one marriage. Many others spend more time in their professional activities to avoid others' company, but destiny makes them more popular than before! In any field they enter, they perform with elegance. What is unknown and mysterious to the multitudes, is easily understood by them.

At the same time, these people expect everyone to follow their version of belief or policy which audacity causes undoing of whatever

77

good they have already accomplished. The hypnotic power bestowed by this 4 & 6 combination may sometimes be misused. In any case, they become trendsetters. They have their own followers who would one day resent their masters' decisions, however deep-rooted their convictions may be. There is one quality that is paramount in all their dealings,-they are seldom tired of experimenting either with their own lives or in their fields of occupation.

What the Number 4 people miss in their personal life, the Number 6 can provide. In spiritual pursuits, Number 6 gives the power of channelizing the powers to reach the ultimate goal. In politics, it helps to create a lasting impression on the minds of even unknown people or people in the distant lands. In society, this combination helps attain an important position in variegated fields. In general, these people evolve policies and concepts and make others follow them. What ails their plans is lack of foresight in sustaining the success!

★ Newsmakers of 4 & 6:

General Charles de Gaulle
(French General who later became the President)

U Thant
(Burmese diplomat;UN Secretary General)

Samuel Beckett
(Irish Novelist)

Joe Louis
(Heavy weight Boxing Champion)

Sarada Devi
(Woman saint of India)

Turgut Ozal
(P.M & President of Turkey)

Louis Vuitton
(Fashion bag designer)

NUMBER 4 - URANUS
BIRTH NUMBER 4 & DESTINY NUMBER 7
(URANUS - NEPTUNE)

The Numbers 4 and 7 are two ends of the same axis. Number 4 represents the head and Number 7 represents the body. As such, one indicates the mental plane and the other, the physical plane. It is needless to say that a "healthy" combination produces great souls on this earth. Usually considered malefic, this combination,if favourably positioned in a natal chart of a person and aspected by benefics, -gives **very great powers and positions in the mundane world which, sometimes cannot be equalled by any other combinations of benefic planets!**

But generally, these Karmic planets have their own ways of helping or harming the natives. Uranus is a diplomat, a politician, an aeronautical or aerospace scientist, a mystic or an intuitive person or a writer who inspires or incites masses. Uranus is signified numerologically by Number 4 and Neptune is a passive follower even as a Destiny Number. If Uranus plays a benefic role Neptune helps the person to channelise the action wisely. If Uranus has a malefic role to play, Neptune shows the person how to escape from the "blame". However, this combination gives a person suspicion, hesitation, agnosticism, relentless search for truth, dogmatic views, cunning, and positively speaking, extreme feelings of patriotism or intelligence.

Some interesting points in the lives of people under 4 & 7 combination are that unexpected changes-good or bad, are common in their lives. On some occasions, even their friends turn enemies and vice versa. Sudden changes in places or countries where they live, unexpected situations in personal life, amassing great wealth unmindful of morals or ethics, or selling commodities or skills which attracts masses instantly are certain common features in the lives of 4 & 7 people. **Name numbers can make the difference!**

Since extreme positions in any aspect of life -such as, marital life, politics, military profession and matters concerning blood relatives may bring harm to self and others; they are advised to "look before they leap"!

79

★ Newsmakers of 4 & 7:

Marcel Dassault

Maria Theresa

Robert P. Wadlow

Yehudi Menuhin

Sir Muhammad Iqbal

Taylor Swift

BIRTH NUMBER 4 & DESTINY NUMBER 8
(URANUS - SATURN)

As a general rule, Number 4 & 8 persons have a turbulent, rebellious and unconventional way of living during their formative years of life. 8 makes the fast-thinking 4 to accept anything only after an analysis. When the No.4 & 8 person gets convinced, he produces the most fascinating or wonderful creation which influences the world for a long time to come.

This 4 & 8 combination is worth discussing only when they are under positive vibrations, because the negative qualities of stubbornness, jealousy, coveting others' money or property and the like should not be bolstered by yet more negative qualities of vindictiveness, delay tactics and ruthlessness. So, when endurance, organising power, energetic work and systematic function are supported by philosophic outlook, analytical approach and society-consciousness, an unforgettable human being is found amidst us. However, 4 & 8 make a good combination - positive or otherwise! (But avoid Number 8 for mundane success).

There are some common traits which both the numbers give. They work hard; some suffer in their childhood either financially or in their intellectual pursuits. Some undertake ventures in faraway lands.

Friends or followers always surround them and pester them for advice or help. The No.4 & 8 persons choose a path or an adventure which many do not dare to venture. Although outwardly they look cool and composed, they are secretive and do not wish others to know what the next move would be. They read a lot and write a lot too. Their chief interest in life is to unearth a treasure or herald a message which was hitherto unknown. The achievements are appreciated during their lifetime and sometimes, it makes them forget what would be in store for them in the womb of future! Hence, it is natural that the Number 4 & 8 people **gamble** in real life! No section of the society can reject their concepts outright. Unfortunately, these people are "conscious" about this fact and yet become self-centered or isolate themselves from their original work or faith wherein they face difficulties. Friends are their assets and family means a different interpretation to them! Mostly they suffer a jolt in business, or health or prestige in later years of life (e.g. Lord Cornwallis!) but the edifice they build will be a landmark in the history. They most probably marry below their status but that no way mars their prestige or stops the flow of luck, -provided the Name Numbers are fine-tuned favourably!

★ **Newsmakers of 4 & 8:**

Pandit Sethuraman
(World-famous Numerologist.)

Dr.John Dee
(Mathematician and Astrologer)

Lord Charles Cornwallis
(British General & Colonial administrator)

Pope Innocent XIII
(Reform -oriented pope of R.C. Church)

Daniel MacMillan
(Scottish Publisher)

T.R.Malthus
(British politician and economist)

BIRTH NUMBER 4 & DESTINY NUMBER 9
(URANUS - MARS)

The combination of Numbers 4 & 9 indicates a Planner - Doer relation. A similar relation is possible between Number 1 & 9. But when **No. 1 inspires, No.4 incites!** Probably, Number 4 people expect faster results and would readily change their plans, professions and strategies. Unlike those under 4 & 8, the 4 & 9 people are more open minded and they function in a level playing field. The initial hesitation and lack of self-confidence of the Number 4 people gets remedied by the aggressive, courageous and dashing 9. That they have secret enemies in their lives is a mystery not yet unleashed!

Though the Number 4 people work more on the mental plane, they do not shirk the physical work. Sportsmen, performing artistes, soldiers and engineers are also commonly found in this group. What impact the Destiny Number 9 causes to a person with Birth Number 4 is a matter of interest. The Martial quality of No. 9 makes the plans of No. 4 a reality. Though astrologically Uranus and Mars are not friendly to each other, when they are under positive vibrations they make a successful team. Individually, or especially as a team the 4 & 9 people excel other combinations under No. 4 to a great extent. The challenges, the losses, and the sufferings do not hamper their progress. Their power of impressing masses is very high. This is not however due to any magnetism or success in secret operations, but purely due to their mental strength fortified by the abnormal courage and endurance. If they are exposed to public life, they may, at one stage, openly speak of their intentions and earn enemies. When their Name Numbers and the dates they choose for their important ventures are lucky, they have their ways and none can stop them. They always work for a group of people or with a group of people. Even those "loners" like scientists, athletes, and writers or poets, either declare their works for the welfare of humanity or their country or form an institution to share their knowledge or skill at one stage or the other during their lifetime. If the Name Numbers are negative, they either suffer personal losses which are irreparable or they become gang lords inflicting losses on fellow-beings.

★ Newsmakers of **4** & **9**:

Francis Bacon

(English statesman; Lord chancellor of England)

Lord Baden Powell

(Founder of the scout movement)

Charles Lindbergh

(American Aviator)

Francisco Franco

(Spanish dictator)

Birju Maharaj

(Kathak dance exponent)

Shakuntala Devi

(Prodigious "human computer")

NAME NUMBERS AND THEIR INTERPRETATIONS

If the value of the letters in your name adds up to number 4, then your name is said to be under the domination of number 4. Let us look into the qualities of those having different name numbers that add up to number 4.

■ Name No.4: As this name number will be only for very short names, it signifies a person or a thing that is popular. It does not bring luck as one might deserve. They will have needless fears, sickness and opposition. They can be well informed and worldly-wise, but still they would work only as subordinates to others.

■ Name No.13: People in the western countries regard this number as unlucky and ominous. They do not stay in rooms or houses having this number and some hotels even do not have rooms with this number. Unexpected events of sorrowful nature occur frequently. Men of this number have bitter experiences and face a lot of difficulties because of women. Though these people do manage to come up in life materially, they would still lead lives full of struggles. This is not a desirable name number. This number gives only severe grief, if birth and destiny numbers are also unlucky.

■ **Name No.22**: The characteristics of those born on the 22nd hold equally good for this Name number also. This number instigates base feelings and emotions. They are drawn towards gambling, drinking, speculation and other vices and will readily indulge in them. They may move towards self-destruction at a great speed and are generally surrounded by wicked and fraudulent people. They invariably earn a bad reputation. They dislike the counsel of others. If the influence of their date of birth is favourable, they can be successful. Otherwise, they have to struggle to prevent total failure. Those with selfish motives invariably urge these people to devious ways in order to further their own interests. They are good administrators and can meet any problem or difficulty with courage. Dangerous circumstances are foreseen. They often face humiliations.

■ **Name No.31**: These people do not care for profit or loss but want only the freedom to do what they desire. Whatever may be the gain involved, they would not like to indulge in anything against their wish. They evince interest in astrology, philosophy and related sciences. These people do not care about what others do or say about them. They only wish to succeed and are never keen on the monetary benefits they gain from such successes. Having succeeded, they sometimes even forgo their due profits. By the 31st year they lose all their material possession and savings. They regain them only by the age of 37. Unexpected happenings will bring about major changes in life. Even their death will be sudden and abrupt. However, when death draws nearer, they somehow become intuitive and sense it well in advance. If their birth number is 1 of any month, this number helps them to achieve great positions in their official career.

■ **Name No.40**: Those under this number earn good friends, who will be of immense help to them in gaining jobs and positions of distinction. It provides accumulation of fine jewellery and wealth. It also brings fame and prosperity. Yet it is their negative qualities that are noticed by others. They can perform any work without any fear. Eventually, their lives will turn out to be fruitless and in vain. They will lose all their money. They will blame the society for not recognizing their services or help. Lot of problems will come up in their lives and the end will be pathetic.

■ **Name No. 49:** This name number brings abundant riches. Their fame will spread far and wide and their achievements will be the envy of others. They lead highly eventful lives and travel a lot. Wonderful experiences, permanent prosperity, excellent properties and sudden fortunes will come to them. Accidents can also happen suddenly. If the birth number is a fortunate one, they lead happy lives. If not, they can end up being hated by others in the society and life will end in a tragic manner. This number kindles the power of imagination.

■ **Name No.58:** This number gives outstanding popularity and the power to captivate others. They are great achievers. Life's progress will be swift. They are pious and orthodox and are great reformers, though attached to religion. If their birth number is 4 or 8 of any month, they will hold positions of great responsibility and fame. They may be sometimes forced to carry out certain things against their wish. Outwardly, these people appear to be very lucky but they also have a lot of unwanted fears within. If the names of those born under other birth numbers also come under this number, life will slowly take a turn for the worse and they will lose their reputation. They may become selfish and may have to undergo a lot of difficulties during their lifetime.

■ **Name No.67:** These people are exemplary artists (they may be artistes who perform) and work with great determination and vigour. They are patronized by power barons and they reveal noble ideas. (**Men should control passions and lust for women.**) Love, affection and grace make these people endearing. They can never achieve anything if they are selfish. This number, which helps to attract and conquer others, does not help non-artists.

■ **Name No.76:** Those having this name number lose all their worldly possessions at some point of time. They are very popular. They will be successful in philanthropic deeds. Surprisingly, they make money in new ways. Income or material gains come through unexpected means. Their last years are generally spent in solitude, doing nothing but eating and sleeping.

■ **Name No. 85:** This name number signifies those who come up the hard way. They not only overcome all afflictions, but help in solving others' problems too. They reveal new ideas about religion and nature. They shine well in the field of medicine. They generally attain a position of distinction and honour.

■ **Name No.94:** These people execute lots of good services for the sake of mankind in general. They bring reforms in society. Comfort and fame will come and go in their lives. Their fame and good work will generally be remembered even after their demise. This is a fortunate name number.

■ **Name No. 103:** This name number is also favourable. There will be improvement in material success initially, followed by a change in business. They will face a lot of competition. Later years will be pleasant and comfortable.

LOVE AND MARRIAGE

FOR THOSE BORN ON THE 4th, 13th, 22nd AND 31st OF ANY MONTH

Uranus is your planet. Their cosmological vibrations affect the mundane world, that is to say, the public life, governments and institutions in such a way that unexpected changes take place mysteriously. So, it is possible that you, born under its influence primarily, are an enigma in your love or marriage to your partner! Revolutionary or unconventional approach to your emotional life may be a common feature. May be you will be in for sudden surprises, pleasant or otherwise, but you know both the cause and the effect!

Your number is 4. It vibrates favourably to the numbers 1, 6, 8 and their series. Those born on such dates attract you and the mutual attraction between you and this lot paves way for a conducive atmosphere to discuss the subject of marriage.

Researching into the numbers of antipathy to number 4, we arrive at the fact that the number that is not fit for a harmonious long term relation is number 4 series itself!

It is found that the numbers 2, 3, 7 and 9 and their series react passively to number 4 and those born on these dates are able to live together with some diplomacy or with adjustments.

MISCELLANY

Since the Number 4 basically signifies the mental faculties and the mundane world, it augments the mental health of self and the people around him. Such persons are capable of curing their physical ailments with their psychic power. If their minds are "unhealthy", their physical health invariably breaks down. Depending upon the Destiny Numbers, the ailments also vary. Yoga, meditation, moderate food habits and keeping off from alcohol and smoking prolong their lifespan.

Their lucky dates are 1st, 10th and 19th of any month. 28th does not confer permanent benefits. If Destiny Number is 1 or 5 for the dates 9, 18 and 27 chosen for any ventures, then favourable results could be obtained. 8, 17, 26 and also 7, 16 are unlucky and dates with such Birth and Destiny numbers should be avoided.

As for any business or profession the Number 4 people choose, hard work is the only key to success. The people under Numbers 1, 2, 4 and 6 (in some cases, 8 also) will be helpful. 2 & 4 also extend help.

MY FORTUNE

They should prefer light blue or yellow when they select their dresses and avoid black. Their lucky gemstones are those with light blue shade. Wearing Hessonite (Gomed) brings good luck and bestows peace of mind.

NUMBERS AND NEWS

Number 4 symbolises the four-fold concept of Divinity in Hinduism; Christianity has 4 prophets in Old Testament and 4 rivers of paradise and also 4 important gospels in the New Testament; Islam refers to 4 Archangels, who are in the service of Allah and also 4 doctrines as its foundation. Science, has its share of the message too! DNA (Deoxyribonucleic Acid) the chief constituent of the genes of any life on this earth (irrespective of religion or race) consists of 4 bio-chemical bases fundamentally!!

NUMBER 5 - MERCURY

People born on day 5, 14 or 23 of any month are ruled by the planet Mercury. If anyone's Destiny Number adds up to a 5, then that person also falls under the influence of Mercury. Mercury is the smallest planet in the solar system and is one of the fastest also. It is called Hermes, Thoth and in Indian system, "Prince". Ancient texts call it the "messenger of Gods". **It is related to the quality of WISDOM.**

Ruled by the planet Mercury, people born under the Number 5 series can be easily recognised. They make friends easily and those under any other Birth or Destiny Number have to reckon with these 5 people. They speak many languages; they practice many trades -just for the sake of it! They are intelligent and quick to understand and do anything which projects them different from others. People from no other number can rebound from worries as fast as No. 5 people do. Just as they befriend people easily, they also give them up if the latter do not suit their "wavelength". Physically and mentally they are agile and somewhat intuitive also. This quality they display in their business or any other activities which involves money. A few of the No.5 people choose fields like astrology, psychology, Tantra Sastra and the like for their profession, since they involve intuition or the mysterious side of mind.

Their minds travel at an immeasurable speed and they evaluate strategies for a business, military operation, matrimonial alliance or organising a public function even before others think of discussing. It is needless to say that there is an inherent risk of "Ignoring an inevitable exigency factor". But, the Number 5 personalities are always willing to take risk in any venture! Thus, when the Number 5 gets connected to a person in any form, it makes him a "gambler", though it may not be always related to speculation with money! Their novel ideas and success-oriented approach in any business effort helps them a lot and they usually strike it rich (Watch their Name Numbers and lucky dates!). However, they invariably do more than one job or involve themselves in more than one profession and find it hard to "sail two boats at a time with one leg in each". If this impractical zeal is kept under control, they hardly fail in their pursuits. There is not a field or subject in the world about which they know nothing. It is because of the innumerable journeys they make in life, or because of their habit of reading or querying about anything and everything. The positive vibrations make them successful in businesses involving, literature, music, travel, stock-broking, journalism, occultism, science or even politics (!). The patriotic ones in such a group become soldiers and freedom fighters.

Those under the negative vibrations of Number 5 and its series become ruthless dictators, revolutionaries, religious bigots and sexual perverts. With some strange numerological influences of Name Numbers and conjunction of planets in the celestial sky, you may find even saints, yogis and world - famous philosophers under the No. 5 series!

They are active, youthful, virile, and mentally agile. Even when they are placed in a grim and precarious situation, they do not forget their humour. In fact, when they have to reply angrily as the situation demands, they use their humour as a weapon! Since these people do not have good control on their emotions (mostly they are "blow hot - blow cold" types!), to be healthy in body and mind, they are advised to be "balanced" in their habits, expressions or feelings and food and pleasures. Now, let us peep into the lives of these Number 5 people with various Destiny Numbers.

NUMBER 5 - MERCURY
What the Birth Dates signify

■ Date - 5   Those who have a message to the world and want to give it fast, unmindful of the impact that it might create, even if it is not palatable, may probably be the persons born on the 5th of any month or its series. Politics, art, music, journalism-be it any field, they have a message so unique and original to give. With the association of some unharmonious destiny and name numbers sometimes, the people born on the 5th might cause confusion, or anarchy. But generally speaking, the whole world would keenly listen to the words of wisdom of the positively charged lot of those born on the 5th and will be immensely benefited. Some undeserving people born on this date of Mercury also shoot to fame (and that is the interesting secret of this number!) but will be exposed very late. Yet, there is also a message! Quickness in understanding or learning, spontaneity in speech and speed in action are their formula to popularity (or even prosperity). However great they may be, at one stage in the lives, they happen to feel that their compatriots or followers have failed to cope with them. On occasions such as that, their religious fervor or belief in the supreme power sustains them. Those with negative destiny and name numbers perish in the race.

■ Date – 14   Travels, varieties of friendships or business associations and help from external sources mark the lives of number 14 people. Taking extreme views does not harm the interests of these people and in fact, this quality eggs them on to achieve greater things. But the success is limited to a season or a specific period. If the "boom period" is exploited (the majority of them certainly do!) without wasting time or resources by those who are born on the 14th, they get catapulted into dizzy heights. They have in their blood the quality of causing a lasting influence on countries, systems, or even on the minds of people. Their lives become history and their deeds become lessons as to what is right and what is wrong. They carve a niche for themselves in any field and out of due respect (or undue fear) they happen to become idols in the society. Some of them give their best for any cause they espouse but the world respects them only after their death. Others who have lucky destiny and name numbers shine in life as pole stars and the posterity worships them. The extremely negative types under this birth date meet with a gruesome end and no force on earth can save them. Success can be achieved and failures can be avoided by prayers in some cases. But as far as the 14th born, they are the masters of their own destiny and they are advised to be vigilant about their own words and actions!

■ **Date – 23**   In whatever field the people born on the 23rd venture, they exhibit a winning streak. So they are believed to be luckier than others. They have a lot of magnetism and are liked or sometimes even adored, even by their adversaries. If destiny and name numbers are favourable they reach the pinnacle of fame and popularity and their followers swell day by day. The learned ones achieve success as poets, industrialists, political leaders and scientists whereas those who did not have a fair amount of formal education also excel in such fields by their sheer wisdom, service to mankind and some unknown skill that is abundant in them! Some people who are not much remembered after their death but have rendered valuable services for a cause (which may draw criticism from some quarters!) also belong to this birth date. Freedom fighters and people who research into the unknown subjects face some controversy at one stage in their lives and fade away temporarily from the annals of history, but resurrect themselves later only to win acclaim and accolades from their countrymen. Among people born on the 23rd, those who lack consistency in their efforts or those who fail to read the minds of fellow humans perish in the race for power and success. Others who are considered lucky attain immortal fame. In general, (with some reservations) the 23rd born, like a few other "naturally lucky" people, provide an interesting study, because they can do a lot for the mankind and also to themselves.

People born under Birth Number 5 (5th, 14th and 23rd of any month) and with various Destiny Numbers will find their lives as follows:

NUMBER 5 - MERCURY
BIRTH NUMBER 5 & DESTINY NUMBER 1 (MERCURY -SUN)

This 5 & 1 combination makes the person lucky. Unlike 1 & 5 (Birth & Destiny Numbers) the person with 5 as Birth Number is luckier in many respects. The authority that is available from the vibrations of Number 1 will boost the image of No. 5 persons. They are actually research -minded and experiment with anything -politics, music, weapons or chemicals, art or occultism. It is because they have a high degree of self-confidence. If the world comes across anything that is modern, sophisticated, or revolutionary in any particular field, it must be the creation of Number 5 & 1 persons only.

Number 5's youthful dynamism matches the majesty of 1 and this combination gives a person a powerful personality. Sometimes, the 5 & 1 lot overemphasize their authority and in the bargain, they are forced to dilute it later. Vehicles, travel and animals offer a lot of fascination for them and they choose their vocations which are in some way connected to these lines only. The positive vibrations of favourable Name Numbers make them VIPs whom the world looks at with reverence. They invent, innovate and introduce new things in the society, which systems or gadgets remain in use for a long time to come. There is something peculiar with this combination: the 5 & 1 persons leave the world with an unfulfilled desire, however rich, powerful or resourceful they may be. You can come to know only if you are close to them. Very rarely, the outside world comes to know about it!

The negative types perpetrate untold atrocities on their adversaries or even on those who oppose their policies. Unlike those positive types of 5 & 1 who are self-effacing and patriotic, the negative ones bring disaster and destruction to their society or country and still they themselves are scarcely affected.

★ Newsmakers of 5 & 1 :

Konrad Adenauer

Akira Kurosawa

Raymond Chandler

Walt Disney

Spencer Tracy

Mobutu Sese Seko

BIRTH NUMBER 5 & DESTINY NUMBER 2 (MERCURY - MOON)

They are good partners while thinking, but not while doing, when it concerns financial matters. The person with 5 & 2 combination is basically a planner since both planets concern MIND. In sports and military the 5 & 2 persons become good strategists; in religion, they introduce doctrines which others may not have even thought of. In politics or statecraft, they only think but are hesitant to execute and need a team of their own to envisage their plan. As architects or industrialists, their mental horizon is so expansive that their designs have a long time impact on the world. In any field where imagination and visualisation are important, their personal skills glitter and they perform better than many of their colleagues. This does not mean that these people work only with their minds. Number 5 is a universal Number and there is not a trade or profession in which you won't find a 5 person! Since the 5 & 2 invariably depends upon good and favourable Name Numbers and lucky dates for their success in life, when they are harmonious by birth or reset numerologically, this combination makes its natives the most successful people in any field!

Since the No. 5 is fast and No.2 is watery, the Number 5 and 2 people must be very careful in taking important decision regarding marriage and the state affairs. They have a poetic skill and a scientific temper and can present the most classic kind of write-ups or records. Their style is unique and even from a poor background they rise to fame meteorically just by their attractive speech and friendly approach. But their moods continuously change and may irritate those who are associated with them professionally or by matrimony. This is especially true in case of people who already live in luxury. That tips the apple cart! So, such people under Number 5 & 2 must understand the team and function or at least they must follow the valuable advice of their benefactors. Caution is your magic potion that saves you from troubles!

★ Newsmakers of 5 & 2:

Bahadur Shah I

John Boyd Dunlop

Colin Powell

Pele

Cecil Rhodes

Chester Bowles

BIRTH NUMBER 5 & DESTINY NUMBER 3 (MERCURY - JUPITER)

Number 5 and 3 are not inimical to each other and this combination gives the person born under its influence a great deal of benefits. The confidence, dignified behaviour, honesty and hard work, and many honourable qualities of Number 3 (Jupiter) will strengthen the inborn shrewdness, diplomatic dealings, intuition, business acumen and adaptability of Number 5 (Mercury). The net result is the most-sought-after human being in any kind of human life. The thirst for details evinced by the 5 & 3 person will make him stand out in any group even if he does not have any formal education or scholastic excellence. It may be due to their power of observation and attractive power of speech or presentation of facts. They are voracious readers and any subject on this earth comes to them easily. They analyse the human behaviour in different angles and the events under different light. So, the revelations which others could not get are easily attained by them. To any walk of life, they add a new dimension. Their thoughts and concepts transcend all barriers and even

95

their adversaries bow their heads to them in secrecy. The harsh reality of this combination is that if their Name Numbers are not harmonious and the efforts taken by them are not noble, then the worst disaster may be in store for them. (To cause a good turn or a bad turn in the history of mankind, Destiny chooses people of certain numbers. This combination is one among them). Unlike the 3 & 5 who are somewhat obstinate in nature and obsessed with their sense of justice, this 5 & 3 are more practical in their approach. Just as 3 & 5 can produce "bad characters" under negative vibrations, 5 &3 also produces such elements that mar the wonderful numerological blend. In such cases, the world gets a message of caution - "Watch your Number!"

There are some peculiar events in the lives of 5 & 3 people. They either lose a limb or spouse or some close friend or relative when they are in the limelight. Some loss, mostly irreparable, remains with them throughout their lives. Most of them are otherwise lucky and have nothing to complain about and they are popular and active in their own spheres of life. Haste or speed beyond a stage - is not their cup of tea! They know it intuitively and do not exceed their known limits. However, they are advised to choose a no-nonsense type spouse, so that the marital life is pleasant. They must keep away from eccentricities of thought and action.

★ Newsmakers of 5 & 3:

Margaret Sanger

Louis XVI

Cristiano Ronaldo

Dr. S.Radhakrishnan

Dakota Fanning

BIRTH NUMBER 5 & DESTINY NUMBER 4
(MERCURY - URANUS)

Though the Number 5 is not generally inimical to other Numbers, the planet Mercury signified by it has an "enemy" in Moon only. As such, the other planets are disposed favourably to it. The people signified by Number 5 & 4 combination are of a strange bondage with destiny. They acquire wealth, power, or popularity by some turn of events unexpectedly. It does not mean they do not deserve the top positions. They have many interests and Number 5 people do not shun any opportunity. If their Destiny Number also favours, they continue discharging their responsibilities. Otherwise, they change their job, premises, position or vocation. Their interest in the ambience, circumstances, co-operation from others and mode of function helps them to become the "best performers" in any field they choose. But, on the other hand, if the conditions are not conducive to envisage their plans, they give up everything and go into "self-exile"! This may be due to the negative "swing" of Uranus (Number 4) which is the Destiny Number.

Owing to the quality of getting displeased with the unfavourable atmosphere very easily, this combination causes disinterest in profession, discontent in married life or seclusion of one kind or the other. At the same time, when the environment is healthy, they take up their responsibilities with renewed vigour and beat all other competitors or rivals hands down. Briefly speaking, these people need a "free hand" to perform. Their individuality and sense of independence make them "freedom-lovers" and their contribution to their country, friends or doctrines they follow is superbly great. When the Name Numbers and dates of action are harmonious, they are lauded for their successful execution of the task. If these governing factors are negative the result is a tragedy. This combination gives good communicating powers and the natives must only learn how to use them to their advantage. If so, they become legends! Religion, fine arts, politics, media or science and technology offer fine opportunities to these people. They should not choose Number 5 people for marriage.

★ Newsmakers of 5 & 4:

King George VI

Harry Cohn

Walter Lippmann

Sir Henry Havelock

J.W.Forrester

Che Guevara

BIRTH NUMBER 5 & DESTINY NUMBER 5 (MERCURY - MERCURY)

Generally, a person's fortune is at the extreme best or at the extreme worst when both his Birth Number and Destiny Number are one and the same. Since, there is no chance of "striking a balance" in such condition to face an emergency, such combinations are viewed unfavourable in classical numerology. But as an exception, 5 & 5 combination bestows positive results. Of course, there is a complementary factor to be additionally considered. That is the Name Number of the native.

The persons under Number 5 & 5 combination are extremely versatile. They are found in more number of fields than the people of any other combination, the reason being that the "universal" or "ubiquitous" nature of Mercury is doubled by 5 & 5. These people have strong minds and an abnormal power. They sometimes behave egoistically (the unbiased observers of these people call it "high handed" also!) and always substantiate their claims with strong evidences and reasons. With positive vibrations, they make efforts to change the erring world in which they live. If they fail, then they use force, - such a force which cannot be ordinarily overcome.

In most of the analyses, they are not presented in "bad light", because the aims of their missions in life are usually noble. With this self-confidence they proceed at "break-neck" speed and achieve their goals. As military leaders they hardly stop conquering countries. As lawyers, they contend in courts vehemently for their cause using all their professional acumen and oratorical skill. As freedom-fighters, they courageously face the might of their adversaries. When it comes to "milder" vocations like art and journalism, they leave no stone unturned to impress the masses by their skills. They expect nothing to stand in their way and are capable of overcoming any kind of hurdles.

It is well-known that Mercury gives a magnetic personality and 5 & 5 combination has abundant magnetism. The majesty of appearance, the humourous presentation of facts, the convincing arguments in any dispute, the skillful handling of any crisis, the "never-say-die" attitude or any such qualities endear them to their countrymen and no doubt they become popular at a very short time in comparison with the people of other numbers. Though they may be successful in their routine lives, there will be some anxious moments too. Overwork, handling too many things at a time, gambling with doubtful situations in business, reckless spending or restless working for others unmindful of one's own health and resources, neglecting priorities of life are some bad qualities which take their toll sooner or later. They must choose a good spouse to take care of their hectic schedule.

★ Newsmakers of 5 & 5:

Augustus Caesar

Haile Selassie

Louis XIV

Sir Archibald Edward Nye

V.O.Chidambaram Pillai

Brij Mohan Khaitan

MY FORTUNE
BIRTH NUMBER 5 & DESTINY NUMBER 6
(MERCURY - VENUS)

A person under this combination of 5 & 6 gives advantageous vibrations to those who have ambitions. The worldly, enthusiastic and dynamic natives under this class reap the reward of their labour. They harvest and enjoy the fruits during their lifetime itself. The hastiness, brash attitude, underestimating others' capabilities and such qualities that mar the personality due to negative vibrations, are adequately "adjusted" to suit the purpose of life, when the Destiny Number of Venus -Number 6, plays its role. At the same time, personal feelings and emotions should not be allowed to overcome the lives of Number 5 & 6 persons, because they land them in trouble. Scandals, humiliation and loss of prestige (the hard-earned one, of course!) are the results of the pre-dominance of Number 6. So, beware!

Though the 5 & 6 natives are found in any profession in which the fate of a multitude of people is at stake (or in a vocation in which only the labour is certain but not the reward), they have a steady and anxiety-free career in the fields of entertainment, hospitality or scientific pursuits. So long as their selfish interests do not hamper their routine work, they continue to rise in their status and financial position. Their magnetic personality and probing minds do their bit and these persons are duly rewarded for their work. Unlike those under this category who are having a greater "positive swing" of Number 5, this lot leads a contented life, even though shifting, unexpected movements and too many involvements (domestic and otherwise) retard their progress.

The upswing in the strength of Number 5 overcomes competition, rivalry, struggles and sacrifices. A kind of uncertainty prevails. But, the "wisdom" associated with the planet Mercury subjects these people to its beneficial vibrations and as such, they steer clear from all the obstacles and achieve their goals. Whatever their careers may be, they become celebrities who give a "healing touch" to the people amidst whom they live. They are dutiful and expect others also to be so. The joke widely quoted about such people - "they are awake even while at sleep!" - is rightly said. But when they really "sleep" in their actions, greater damages are done by the all-powerful Destiny and the loss becomes irreparable. However, they have a wonderful mass appeal and command influence at all levels. There is one great quality that makes them stand out in a crowd of numerological luminaries, -that is, their high degree of flexibility and understanding the priorities of human life. They suffer jolts in their family life, but they recover fast, because they understand the vagaries of fate. Those among this lot who lack such a philosophic outlook of life become victims of the extreme emotions and do eccentric things. But for the initial struggles and wanderings of both mind and body, this combination seems to be a fine one.

⭐ Newsmakers of 5 & 6:

Albert Einstein

Edward VIII

Alan Turing

Dwight D.Eisenhower

Julie Christie

Sir Gilbert Parker

BIRTH NUMBER 5 & DESTINY NUMBER 7 (MERCURY– NEPTUNE)

Mercury and Neptune, represented by Numbers 5 and 7 respectively are friendly to each other. To be more accurate, we must say Neptune or Number 7 is "not as much friendly" towards Mercury. As such, in certain matters connected to philosophy, occultism, the power of healing, biosciences and dramatics, Number 7 will be of good use to Number 5. They foresee or imagine many things even before they happen, although they may not recognize their own powers. This is to some extent true in the case of Number 5 also. But, when negative vibrations predominate, the Number 5 & 7 person becomes over-imaginative thus missing the element of logic and practicality. As a result, they are feared! Still, they have their own followers who are struck by the magnetic character of 5 & 7 and help the common cause upheld. The doctrines and theories of the positively united 5 & 7 person bring him honour, popularity and wealth whereas under negative waves the same person may cause a great damage to himself and all those around him! **Beware!** "**Mr.5&7**", you must choose a very lucky date for marriage!!

If the world needs someone to entertain, educate or lead with foresight, 5 & 7 is the right person to do it. Interestingly, all subjects under the sun are their cups of tea! The vibrations of Number 7 give a kind of detachment and in most of the cases, the people of this combination do not concentrate much on their domestic life. The routine of everyday life takes them to distant places or keeps them apart from kith and kin. In the commonly found 5 & 7 groups, I have come across people who do not have time to rest, recuperate or spend time with their children, even though they are good entertainers in public life or fine conversationalists in private. It is a matter of surprise that they know well what the world needs, but they need someone else to take care of their "own" needs! Incidentally, they are not like the ones under the Number 3 series (especially those under Name Number 12) who would always be ready to forgo their own comforts for a larger cause. Well, that's 5 & 7 type! If the shortcomings mentioned in the said study are overcome, then there is a wonderful soul amidst us who guides us to liberation from not only the worldly problems, but also from the problems haunting our souls. He cures us of our diseases, relieves us of our gloom, tickles our ribs making us laugh heartily and lulls us to sleep peacefully! Even "serious" personalities under 5 & 7 exhibit their "lighter vein", if given an opportunity. Since their minds are continually milling "thoughts" only in the interest of others' causes or problems, they are advised to take the drug which they prescribe to others and watch the difference. In addition, Yoga and Meditation will cause miracles to happen!

★ Newsmakers of 5 & 7:

William Shakespeare

K.G.Gillette

Emmeline Pankhurst

Karl Landsteiner

Roger Moore

F.A.Mesmer

Eamon de Valera

BIRTH NUMBER 5 & DESTINY NUMBER 8 (MERCURY - SATURN)

As much as Number 5 is welcome, Number 8 is dreaded and avoided by many people. Their fears are not unfounded. The Karmic planet Saturn represented by Number 8 in Numerology is a **strict judge.** He delivers judgements without fear or favour when he deals with the lives of the earthlings. Combined with a neutral like Number 5, sometimes Number 8 gives a dual nature to the people of this combination. So, when 5's vibrations are synchronised with those of 8, the person is steady in his thought, careful in his words and judicious in his actions. Otherwise, conflict arises and hell breaks loose! So, choose favourable Name Numbers always.

The basic quality of Number 5 is their "mercurial" temperament whereas that of Number 8 (especially when it comes as a Destiny Number) is pessimistic hesitation. When No. 5 is an extrovert, No 8 prefers solitude. Though the numerological disparities make the person under the combined vibrations of 5 & 8 pulled by two forces in opposite directions, Number 8 balances the situation and the person attains self-realisation. Those who come under the "negative" current of Saturn become selfish, destructive, sinful and pave way for their own ruin and that of others who are dependent on them. The children born under this combination should be brought up with care so that the "negative" qualities of both 5 and 8 do not take roots in their personality. Philosophic attitude during failures or suffering, courage in the face of opposition, daring at the moment of danger, unsagging spirit in the toughest quest for truth and extra caution before taking a monumental decision are the welcome qualities of a "positively disposed" 5 & 8 person.

The only advice that these people should follow is: "Bend your body; Mend your mind; end all evil thoughts and desires!" This formula alone can lead them to successful and happy life. If still some mishaps like litigation, spouse's ill-health and professional rivalry torment this 5 & 8 people, it is because they are inescapable victims of Karma and must face them with prayers to the Almighty! Many of them become famous for their clairvoyance or their rule by law or strange scientific inventions.

The combination of 5 & 8 as Birth & Destiny Numbers has produced great lives that uplifted the mankind (though some "negative" types walked on this earth). Here are a few:

★ Newsmakers of 5 & 8:

Michel De Nostradamus

Adlai Ewing Stevenson

Gerald Ford

Francois Duvalier "Papa Doc"

Gregory Peck

Rex Harrison

BIRTH NUMBER 5 & DESTINY NUMBER 9
(MERCURY - MARS)

To Mercury, Mars is not inimical but to Mars, Mercury is an enemy. This is the relation chart given by occultism. Mercury as the Birth Number and Mars as the Destiny Number, signify a pair one of which is moist and chill and the other one is combust and hot. Indeed it is a surprise that the pair works well!

Number 5 & 9 combination represents a person who is discreet but stern as well. He is soft but strong. He has common sense and cannot be taken for a ride. He may be god-fearing, but is aware that God acts only through men. He is elastic but would snap at any time. He thinks tediously but acts expeditiously. He is imaginative, but in action very practical.

There are some peculiarities with this Number combination. Those who come under this category enjoy the fruits of their background or labour and also suffer by a quirk of fate. They write a lot and tear the write-ups sometimes. They could earn a lot of money but still long for spending what they have. They change places and plans often yet they achieve fame. When they are at work, they brook no opposition or interference. Some even do not care for good advice! When they take a vow, they fulfill it perfectly - even for a wrong purpose. If they lead a saintly life, they are embodiments of immaculate morality. If they lead a wayward life, their end will be the most tragic. Many of these people who took up noble causes became praiseworthy citizens. On the other hand, those who ignored moral values and human concerns died ignominiously. However, all of them had one quality in common, ---fighting stoically against odds!

This category also needs to reset the spellings of their names, if one after another failures and sufferings occur in their lives. Their aims must be noble and for a good cause. Otherwise, they take off to dizzy heights of status and power and without a warning, they may be dropped to the earth by destiny. This is what Numerology does to bad people with lucky numbers! Somehow, under this category, those who do not follow the red signals in the traffic of life, meet with fatal accidents from which they seldom recover. Those who judge their moves and follow a path of sacrifice for their fellow-beings are safe and sound and also find a decent place in the history.

Political alliances, marriage, business partnerships and uniformed services are to be dealt with utmost caution and care. No doubt, Numbers rule the world, but if there is a slip, they will "fool" the world also! This must be remembered.!

★ Newsmakers of 5 & 9:

Guy de Maupassant

Albert Schweitzer

Abul Fazl

Ray Kroc

Joseph Lister

NAME NUMBERS AND THEIR INTERPRETATIONS

If the sum total of the values of letters in a name adds up to 5, then it is said to be under the influence of this number which represents the planet Mercury.

■ **Name No.5:** This number gives the power to charm people, exude dynamism and to lead a luxurious life enjoying fame and prominence. They spend money lavishly. These people should cultivate perseverance and concentration of mind.

■ **Name No.14:** This number is suitable for trade. Those having this Name number are always surrounded by a lot of people and things. They are successful in various trades and will meet a lot of friends. They may have strange problems and may face disappointments by trusting others. They may also face risk from thunder, lightning, water and fire. They undertake frequent travels. These people are advised to be careful while travelling in fast-moving vehicles. If the product in which they trade also comes under number 14, it will have excellent public patronage. The matters concerning love and marriage must be considered and reconsidered many times before a decision is taken. If not, these people may marry in haste and repent at leisure. This number can be called a very lucky number.

■ **Name No.23:** This number is the luckiest of all Mercury (5) numbers. These people find success in all their endeavours. All their plans will succeed. They can achieve things which others won't even imagine. Their accomplishments will astonish those around them. In spite of being such lucky people, if they do not strive hard, they would be enjoying luxuries that they are not worthy of. Since they succeed in all their efforts, they will earn the patronage, respect, honour and favour of people in very high positions. Hence, these people are advised to keep up high standards and work out plans to achieve their goals. If not, they might end up leading lives of luxury and pomp devoid of any personal accomplishment. The positive types among them are the most-sought-after type executives in governments or in private enterprises. The negative types devote time to sleep and day-dreaming.

■ **Name No.32:** This number can attract a variety of people. They have a mass appeal and they come out with unique ideas and techniques even without prior experience. This potent and forceful number can make anyone a prominent person. If they lead their life exploiting their intuition, life will be wonderful. If they listen to the advice of others, failures may recur one after another. This number is said to be the epitome of wisdom and intuition. They have above-average intelligence and a witty manner of speaking. They will become geniuses. Ups and downs will be common in their lives. They will attain high positions in life and will be youthful in appearance even in old age.

■ **Name No.41:** This number denotes the qualities of charming and controlling. They are renowned achievers and they have high ideals. They are keen about their development and will be world-famous. When they become heady with success, they get into things or matters which are beyond their capability. The failures that could result from such situations will be cleverly hidden from the public scrutiny. They are found to lead successful lives.

■ **Name No.50:** They are very intelligent people and analyse everything thoroughly. They excel in education. Some people will shine as good teachers. Some others use their intelligence to make money. They are lucky after the age of 50. Their life span will improve and they live longer.

■ **Name No. 59:** Similar to persons belonging to number 50, these people are also research-minded. Their writings are full of humour and they would shine as "Humour Kings" among writers. They would become rich by writing and get excellent public support. Their aim will be to earn money. They will enjoy permanent fortunes. They may suffer from nervous diseases including paralysis. Hence, it is necessary for them to have good habits and keep themselves healthy.

■ **Name No.68:** This number is lucky to a certain extent. However, life that starts quite pleasantly may suddenly grind to a halt. They will get involved in schemes that they cannot execute and will be badly hurt. Their greed will spoil their career and life. The fortunes that came through an unforeseen stroke of luck may soon disappear. Hence, this number is not quite fortunate.

■ **Name No.77:** This number denotes sincere effort, self-confidence and hard work. Support from others brings in profits, fame and honour. Life will be very enchanting. They reap full benefits of this number only if they repose faith in god. They get chances to travel aboard.

■ **Name No. 86:** This number denotes those who come up in a gradual manner and the hard way. They get what they deserve. They earn the favour and help of rich people. With the help so received, they will lead comfortable and happy lives. They will have good savings and lead happy lives.

■ **Name No. 95:** This number signifies a disciplined life combined with daring events and honour. They are successful in trade and achieve distinction. By trading in a variety of new things, they amass wealth. They are excellent orators and will become popular in their line of business.

■ Name No. 104: This number will bring success in life followed by unexpected changes. Though they can be good achievers, they can only earn fame and not money. In other words, they become popular but material success may be a far cry.

LOVE AND MARRIAGE

FOR THOSE BORN ON THE 5th, 14th AND 23th OF ANY MONTH

Mercury is your planet. It is a very fast moving planet in the solar family. Believed to be the "messenger of gods", this planet and the number 5 that signify it are related to human wisdom. Since the people born under this number are commonly found in any group, it is called a "universal number". As its name implies, it is friendly with people born on any date and can be considered for love or any serious relationship or marriage, although there are some exceptions.

Your number is 5. Your vibrations allow you to be attracted by those born on the 5th and 9th and their series.

Those born on the dates of 1, 2, 3, 4, 6, 7 and 8 may react passively to your number and may be chosen as spouses. All that you should ensure is that you both have harmonious name numbers.

The interesting aspect of these dates of 5 is that those born under its influence are not antipathic towards any others for love or marriage, although harmonious name numbers play a positive role.

MISCELLANY

Number 5 people (also applicable to those with Destiny Number 5) find 5th, 9th, 14th, 18th, 23rd and 27th of any month as lucky days. One peculiar trait with Number 5 is that all numbers adjust themselves favourably with 5. But marriage dates falling on any date adding up to a 5 must be avoided.

As for profession, these people can take up all new ventures on any Birth date of 5, 14 or 23. If the Destiny Number falls under 1 or 3, it is very good for the future. Persons born under Numbers 1, 4, 5 or 9 also are good for partnerships. These 5 people should not jump often from one job to another, though they have a strong desire to do it.

Always check your Name Numbers and reset, if necessary.

Ash colour or Grey is the luckiest one. Any light colours would suffice while choosing a dress. Dark colours especially dark green and black should be avoided. The best gemstone suitable for these people is Diamond or Zircon.

NUMBERS AND NEWS

Numerologically discussing, **PENTAGON** which is the nerve-Centre and pride of America's global military might was **always** vulnerable to attack!

USA's ruling sign of Zodiac is **Gemini**. It is ruled by **MERCURY** which is represented in Numerology by **Number 5** which is also the Destiny Number of the fateful day in U.S. history, i.e. **11th September, 2001** (1+1+9+2+1 = 14 = 5). The twin towers looking like two 1s placed side by side (they are not connected by a strong cross construction to look like H which represents 5). The two "ones" add to a 2 which represents **Moon** which is the only planet astrologically inimical to **Mercury (or Number 5)** WTC suffered the terrorist attack first! And the worst ever too...!!

Incidentally, Pentagon, having 5 sides 5 floors, 5 main administrative wings and covering 5 acres suffered the attack. 5 did not suffer as much as 11 suffered!

This gory incident cannot be a co-incidence!!

110

NUMBER 6 - VENUS

Venus is called *SUKRA* in Indian texts. It governs the refined feelings of human beings like their romance, music, poetry, love or passion, artistic sensibilities and physical attraction. As regards the anatomy, it represents eyes, kidney and reproductive system of human beings. Venus, if favourably posited in a natal chart and aspected beneficially, gives an attractive personality, skill in fine arts, and a comfortable life with all the luxuries thereof. Since Venus is the lord of Tantra, Space, the written word, research, mystic religious pursuits, music, hospitality and even "secret" military strategies, the people who are born under the Birth Numbers of Venus, viz.,. 6th, 15th and 24th are found in any one or more of the fields said above (Even Destiny Numbers too!)

Venusians are considered fortunate, because they are welcome in any company or business. Their appearance, way of dressing, aesthetic sense, hypnotic talk, physical beauty (sometimes sex appeal!) and influential connections add a new dimension to all walks of human life. The positive influence of Venus makes one a remarkable human being whom the world would adore and worship. If negative influences dominate, he becomes a despicable character whom the world hates and shuns. There is one marked difference between the negative Venusians and the negatively charged persons of other Numbers. Number 6 people's negative qualities cannot be easily recognized by the people around them. They could be TWO PERSONALITIES, within and without. You would never know it unless you experience it! It is easy to identify the intentions of the persons of all the other numbers but it takes some time or experience to learn fully the personality of Number 6! This is the only category in the realm of Numerology found to "enjoy life" (it does not mean anything sensual always; it could be spiritual enjoyment also). That is to say, when the people under all the other Numbers find their lives boring or monotonous at one stage or the other, the Number 6 people find it interesting and eventful even if they happen to live solitarily in an uninhabited island! Well, these are the people who first choose to leave the "world" all of a sudden (or to become recluses), when they feel that the world has nothing to offer. Such people under Number 6 are in some way associated with the negative vibrations of their Birth and / or Destiny Numbers. It's time they watch their marital life too!

(A detailed study of the Number 6 people is available in the pages of "SCIENCE OF FORTUNE" by the same author).

Number 6 also consists of many "Swashbucklers" both on the screen and in real life. Once they decide to achieve something, they stop at nothing! They do not spare their targets. Be it pen or gun, they try whatever they have in their hands! If you carry out a research as to who figures in the newspapers regularly, that too in large numbers, you will invariably come across Number 6 people only. They are born "newsmakers" and without them there will be no romance or spice in the life on our earth! If deceit, immoral practices and scant regard for fellow humans could be kept off, Number 6 the Venusians, would emancipate the whole world from its sufferings and add succour to the life.

In general, the Number 6 is conducive to get progeny (Some "Sixers" have more number of children than others!) Some of the "Six" personalities perform extraordinary feats in life and find their names enshrined in the history!

What the Birth Dates signify

■ Date - 6   This Venusian date of birth has not only produced famous nation builders, artists, writers, and politicians but also the first Indian test tube baby! They have some feminine traits or they are attracted towards opposite sex. Subtle things in life catch their attention and they usually fall for beautiful designs and externally attractive ideas. They have a unique style in handling whatever objects or jobs they do. Their keen intellect is thirsty for opportunities and so the mission that they venture into may be noble or otherwise. A good number of them depend upon a team of advisors and that might cause a disaster in some cases. In statecraft, they embark upon some plans unmindful of the risks involved and either they lose the battle or win a pyrrhic victory. Many under this date of this birth choose easy careers (to avoid controversies) such as, painting, poetry or theatre and they excel in them. Politicians born on this date, though initially successful, are bound to get into trouble in the later half of their life. Those with a noble cause and good destiny and name numbers shine so well, that they become heroes in the history. Others whose only policy is greed and high-handedness soon meet their doom. A few of this lot, when they perish due to a quirk of fate, certainly evoke sympathy. The only secret of the successful people of this category is that they are perfect strategists!

■ Date – 15   In general, the people born on the 15th have the knack of attracting the world's attention. It may be due to the beauty of their physique, thoughts and deeds or even their wealth! (The women born on this date are reportedly rather attractive than their male counterparts!) They retain their youthfulness even after aging. As kings or heads of state, they do not permanently enjoy the victories they won until their end. So is the case of political leaders, military leaders and social activists. Either the mood of the public swings in favour of the opponents or death overcomes them. But the people connected to the fields of art, theatre, business and industries seem to have longer innings. Some of the people of the latter category even find sudden fortunes! Scientists and engineers, who are capable of maintaining cordial relationship with the administrator, (may be, by using the charm of their birth date and favourable name number!) are amply benefited. The skill of oration of these people or their powerful writings, attract the masses. Depending upon the strength of their destiny and name numbers their success in any particular field is determined. The way this Venusian date and the supporting numbers influence the world, will prove whether the people born on this date survive the onslaught of time or not. Those born on the 15th are advised to be cautious when they are on a foreign soil or dealing with alien cultures, as their charm may run out!

■ Date – 24   If most of the Venusians are said to possess some natural charm that captivates the hearts of the people at home or abroad, it is correct to a great extent in the case of those born on the 24th! Maybe they have a strong reason too. Great entertainers, sports personalities and adventurists, if born on the 24th, are assured of success. Some people born on the 24th take to pen or brush and paint and attain phenomenal success. Generally, these Number 24 people get a lot of favours from the governments or win public acclaim, although those among them with a weaker "swing" of the number meet with disastrous ends to their career or life. Studying their lives thoroughly, one has to conclude that the charm or popularity of those born on the 24th is not through any natural phenomenon, but only due to their clear thinking and careful execution of their plans. (That is why I am unable to assert unequivocally that the birth date 24 is "100% lucky", because they really deserve the praise!) There may be saintly characters born on this date. Interestingly, they are not like their counterparts under Number 3 whatever course their lives take. It is sure that these people's "charm" or influence lasts even after their death!

People born under Birth Number 6 (6th, 15th and 24th of any month) and with various Destiny Numbers will find their lives as follows:

BIRTH NUMBER 6 & DESTINY NUMBER 1 (VENUS -SUN)

One of the eventful lives under the Number 6 series belongs to those born under Number 6 & 1 combination. The inborn magnetism of Number 6 combined with the leadership qualities of Number 1 helps them achieve an indelible image in the history of mankind.

These people do not find their lives easy and comfortable during their childhood. If they were born rich, then they would be found resenting the regimentation they are put under. They struggle, but struggle elegantly. They put forward their arguments in a flamboyant but powerful style. Their enemies too will have a high regard for their intelligence and leadership, but will not openly express their opinion, however secretly they may be plotting. Some of the Number 6 people become "narcissists" and forget that they may have to blame themselves one day for not paying much attention to the plans of their adversaries. But, mostly they are on the alert and may not suffer easily at the hands of destiny. They have to safeguard themselves from "under-estimating" the hurdles on their path. If it is taken care of, there is no failure in their history. Many under Number 6 come to be understood and worshipped only after they leave this world. Either they do not generally have marital fidelity or suffer from some anxiety about their children. That does not stop them from marching ahead in the path of victory until, one day, when they are still trying to complete their mission, Destiny packs them off! These Number 6 & 1 lot mostly earn fame and popularity far away from the places of their origin or birth. Their doggedness, foresight and even failures will become lessons to the posterity for centuries to come. However hardened and rugged they may seem to be outwardly either in their policies or behaviour, they have a soft heart which has many sweet secrets to share in privacy. Anyhow, for success 6&1, people should have a good Name Number!

The Number 6 & 1 types mentioned below are worthy of research by any student of Numerology, whether they belong to the positive or negative type:-

★ Newsmakers of 6 & 1:
Steve Jobs
Nero
Sir Ernest Shackleton
Napoleon Bonaparte
Dr.Martin Luther King Jr

MY FORTUNE

Mario Puzo.

BIRTH NUMBER 6 & DESTINY NUMBER 2
(VENUS - MOON)

The people signified by 6 & 2 have conflicting vibrations. If Venus is predominant in its positive aspect, even if the Moon causes some anti-vibrations, it may not affect this combination much. Partnerships for a long term and eternal bonds (in a tolerant society, it means also a sustained married life) are not quite advisable. However, for ad hoc or casual arrangements, choosing a lucky Number 2 in terms of Name Number or dates for auspicious purposes must be agreeable.

Thespians, poets, romantic writers, businessmen dealing in cosmetics and things worn next to our skin, politicians who change sides (those who do not change suffer silently!), stock-brokers, educationists, public relations experts and of course, rank opportunists (!) are the people who are mostly topping this particular category of Number 6 series. They are worldly, sagacious and influential in the society.

The basic qualities of 6 (or Venusians) are nevertheless affected by the Destiny Number 2. Changes in moods or fortunes, laziness, refraining from action when necessary, following no fixed rules to satisfy selfish ends, commanding others (or cleverly convincing) to do the work for own benefit and sometimes, involvement in scandals concerning opposite sex, following impracticable ways to enforce rules are some defects of this Number 6 & 2 combination. If these are avoided in routine life, the natives can avoid losses of prestige, mental peace, status and health.

Those who are stung by the positive influence of 6 & 2 are generally finding themselves at cross roads of destiny with vacillating minds, not knowing what to do and which road to choose. They act by their conscience or as per a divine dictate. Even if they face problems, they have a philosophic attitude which comforts them and helps them to forge ahead. They become the embodiment of love and compassion and the humanity does not forget them.

★ **Newsmakers of 6 & 2:**

Hadrian

Pushkin

John Sutter

Zafarullah Khan

Ronald Reagan

Tony Blair

A.R.Rahman

Edward Bach

BIRTH NUMBER 6 & DESTINY NUMBER 3
(VENUS - JUPITER)

Immanuel Velikovsky, a modern astronomer claimed that Venus was ejected from the gaseous atmosphere of Jupiter so many thousands of years ago and having roamed the solar system as a comet for several years, settled into the planetary orbit. This theory of "evolution amid catastrophe" is now an accepted theory. But, Venus (closer to earth comparing Jupiter) somewhat akin to Moon, is astrologically considered to pass negative radiations to JUPITER. Mythology depicts them as two teachers, each having his own group of pupils, having opposite interests.

This combination gives its natives many opportunities to excel in personal and mundane lives. They are perfectionists and ambitious. They have an ideal view of life. Heights, literally speaking, are of great interest to them. Aeroplanes, high-rise buildings or sky scrappers, soul's journey to heaven, space and the places beyond it, wild imagination, tall trees, big plans or big money, lofty ideals and extreme emotions, ... all these things or one of these things will become their life's craze. They are strong personalities but they sometimes concentrate more on the superstructure of the edifice they build and forget the strength of the foundation. This creates some obstacles in their personal lives or careers. Their fast thinking and

117

quick responses cannot be matched by others and this trait also becomes a bone of contention. Since Number 6 and Number 3 emanate conflicting vibrations, the persons born under this combination are a puzzle even to their own selves. That does not mean they are unable to solve the puzzle or mystery related to others or other domains. This group of people has the highest degree of cognition and intelligence and it is possible that this gift makes them victims of their own virtues. In addition, at one stage or the other in their lives, the quirk of fate causes some kind of loss to them and it remains an indelible scar throughout their lives. If their freewill could be bolstered by a philosophic outlook or by prayers, they overcome the same easily. Otherwise, they succumb to the feelings of loss or agony. Numerology can unearth the causes and their remedy very well.

There is some deficiency in their lives due to non-synchronisation of Name Numbers and dates of birth. But Freewill, in many ways helps the people and NUMBERS may help them to lead a complete life! ... Remember! They are born achievers with a strong sense of commitment of their cause.

★ Newsmakers of 6 & 3:

Sir Walter Scott

Queen Victoria

Sir Stamford Raffles

Sachin Tendulkar

Bachendri Pal

(First Indian Woman to Conquer Mt.Everest).

BIRTH NUMBER 6 & DESTINY NUMBER 4
(VENUS- URANUS)

If you find someone "awake while at sleep", please ask him his date of birth. It is probable his Birth Number is 6 and Destiny Number is 4. But such people are not somnambulists. To be awake while at sleep, to laugh while in grief, to revel forgetting to regret, to relax when one has to act ----You can go on describing the 6 & 4 characters in the aforesaid manner. These intelligent and intuitive persons possess an abnormal mental strength which keeps their fertile minds awake and alert. Their vivid dreams sometimes come true! Physically or mentally they are always prepared to work hard. Generally they do not get alarmed easily in the event of any emergency. They are skilled in many subjects and crafts and some of them are so highly skilled in their fields that the governments and world bodies shower honours and awards on them. Research proves that most of the people under this 6 & 4 combination live longer than many of their counterparts under different numbers. The "effect" is known, but not the "cause" and that is why we may have to classify this combination as a "KARMIC" group!

Like some Numbers, these people are not "square pegs in round holes". They have a definite aim from their early days of life and even if they make a decision in their middle age, they put their hearts and souls into that plan and come out successful. The courtesy, pleasing manners, captivating looks and powerful speech, readiness to work hard, intuitive planning and facing challenges with smiles are their stepping stones to success. In their service to humanity they are second to none and their concern for the suffering masses or for their country's development transcends all the conventional barriers. There is something "ominous" too in this 6 & 4 combination. Not all get away with their misdeeds, if any they do, due to negative vibrations of numbers and the damage done or punishment awaiting will be an unprecedented one! Beware, you 6 & 4! Safeguard yourself from over confidence and over-enjoyment of life.

Money, Royal or Government patronage, people who praise, friends and fans to follow and popularity or successful lifestyle are usually accepted by these 6 & 4 personalities in a philosophical manner. Those who become intoxicated by the fame and accolades they receive, will have a tragic downfall from which they hardly recover. If this tendency has been overcome, they live longer and stronger and become legends during their own life time. Please remember, my dear 6 & 4 friends! When you

119

forget God, God also forgets you!

★ **Newsmakers of 6 & 4:**

Leonardo Da Vinci

Sigmund Freud
(Austrian psychoanalyst of fame)

Warren Hastings
(Governor General of India; impeached)

Steve McQueen

Mohammad Zahir Shah
(deposed Afghan King)

M.S.Oberoi

Le Corbusier

BIRTH NUMBER 6 & DESTINY NUMBER 5 (VENUS - MERCURY)

Mutually friendly, Venus and Mercury confer good results to those born under Numbers 6 and 5 respectively as Birth and Destiny Numbers. This combination is of great interest to professional numerologists also because these people easily derive the "positive" benefits of their governing planets. At least *outwardly* it seems so, because *inwardly* how they labour hard and how they achieve position may not be known to the outside world! The slow, manipulative, and romantic Venus coupled with the fast, versatile and rational Mercury, cause miracles in the lives of these natives. Since this combination helps them get the fruits of their labour during their very lifetime, it evokes interest. (If anyone under this combination is not found "lucky", you may summarily decide that the Name Number of the person must be disharmonious to a very great extent).

Number 6 representing Venus, usually widens the mental horizon of the natives, especially that of those who possess it as their Birth Number. Coupled with the fast-acting and intelligent Mercury as the planet of their destiny, they master any subject on the earth. To achieve their ends, they would use any method good or bad, and the result is usually favourable. Many successful people who are of this category have vividly explained in secrecy that they followed a policy, "Ends justify means!" to become popular and rich!

However, it does not mean that they are bad. They think, plan, organise, gamble, establish, manage and enjoy their professions or activities of their own choice. There is a peculiar trait in their personality -they are readily accepted in the society or by the world at large. No land is foreign to them and no person is inconvincible. If they have enemies, they are "sworn enemies", but their adversaries fail to contain them easily. Revolution has a strange but benevolent interpretation in their lives. Many of them are found fighting for somebody else's causes. Those who have a background of their own, -surprisingly, find it difficult to maintain it. The only solace in many of these cases is that they cleverly hide their feelings and smile cheerfully and make the best use of their resources to overcome their obstacles. In their private lives, not much will be known, sometimes even to their own near and dear ones. (This may be a common phenomenon with a couple of other Numbers also, but this is a special case!) The favourable vibrations of this combination help them to reap the harvest of their untiring efforts and the fruits are shared by the posterity for a long time to come. The negative ones cause destruction and anarchy at various levels of human life, although they themselves escape by "surf-riding" the issues. Some even become victims of their own policy!

As related earlier, this very interesting numerological combination is fit for research. Now, meet the fascinating people born under Number 6 & 5 given here below:

★ Newsmakers of 6 & 5:

Lord Alfred Tennyson

Azim Premji

Alexander Fleming

Max Muller (Oxford professor of German origin)

Lee Iacocca (Chrysler Corporation's Chairman)

Ernst H.Heinkel

MY FORTUNE

Simon Bolivar ("The great liberator")

Gustave Eiffel (Designer of Eiffel Tower)

BIRTH NUMBER 6 & DESTINY NUMBER 6 (VENUS - VENUS)

The fact that like poles repel each other is not always applicable to this combination. Since 6 and 6 could in many ways "attract" each other and so, conclusively we cannot rule that they are "repelling" each other. For instance, a Number 6 & 6 man invented the game of basketball and another Number 6 man born 24 years later made it an Olympic sport. The 6 digit PIN code was introduced in India on the sixth of a month and the date's Destiny Number was also a 6. It was cleared after a lot of deliberations by a group of 6 experts. Both the systems are popular and have survived the onslaught of time! An expert Numerologist will always back his predictions by thorough analysis and research and will prove that a benefic or malefic Number is not **always** of such nature and its quality varies depending upon certain parameters. 6 & 6 combination is one such pair! However, these lovers of nature, pets and fine arts are quizzical personalities also!

Numbers 6 & 6 representing Venus -Venus combination has been adjudged to possess the quality of a **Sine Wave** of electric current. It has two peaks, one is positive; the other one is negative. Depending upon the direction of the "swing", your fortunes also vary. The intricacies of Venus -Venus combination are so strange that these people who achieve their lofty goals so easily in their professional lives are not favourably disposed in their personal lives. No doubt, they are popular, friendly, mostly rich, influential and intelligent. But emotions and societal considerations overcome their professional or political compulsions. When artists, writers and the like express their feelings and ideas in their own style, they win acclaim. But, others who are capable of influencing the opinion or lifestyles of the ordinary citizens express their ideas and unfold their actions, find a lot of opposition in the offing. Who cares? A Venusian, though dependent on his skill of garnering public support for implementing his schemes, forgets for a while the cardinal principle of his number and goes into action, -a strong action, because his destiny number is a 6. It is a matter of interest that the same 6 & 6 person may "swing" to the opposite side and shelve his "bravado" silently! That is 6 & 6!

Spouse, children, pets, servants, in general those under the care of Number 6 & 6 persons resent the moods of the latter and cause an anxiety at one stage. Research proves that there is some domestic unhappiness which may make the relations "break" instead of "bending". Caution is necessary, when important or secretive plans and schemes are discussed with the subordinates or colleagues, because the integrity of such people may prove to be doubtful in future.

There is a peculiarity with this particular combination. However upright and religious they may be, these "strong" Venusians are at loggerheads with Destiny one day and they might feel that God has "forsaken" them! If we observe from a neutral stand point, we can understand that this particular group lacked tact and foresight in their actions; hence their pitfall! The successful ones achieve their aims, because by nature or by choice their Name Numbers and dates they have chosen happen to be harmonious leading to success. The unsuccessful ones are those who never sought "proper" advice. It is yet another matter, whether they had any good advisers at all, although the people of this number are always surrounded by friends, patrons or followers.

Some prominent people under the combination of 6 & 6 as Birth & Destiny Numbers are given here for the benefit of readers and enthusiasts:

★ **Newsmakers of 6 & 6:**
 Galileo Galilei
 Joan of Arc
 William Pitt, the Elder (P.M. of Britain)
 Sylvester Stallone
 Dame Agatha Christie (Detective fiction writer)

Bjorn Borg (Tennis Champin)

George Bush Jr.

BIRTH NUMBER 6 & DESTINY NUMBER 7
(VENUS – NEPTUNE)

The alchemy of Numbers 6 and 7 consists of friendly vibrations relating to public speaking, writing poems and novels, histrionics, working in places away from the place of birth and habits of meditation and probing into the unknown. Many people who belong to this category are generally men of words or letters. The exceptions can boast themselves of possessing poesy or histrionic talents.

The positive types have a wonderful doctrine to tell the world. They have a charming countenance and hypnotising power of speech which help them reach the position of a leader or a literary giant. Even their writings will not be always a "serious" type and so it entertains everyone. The political leaders, who use their glib of the tongue or their mighty pen, usually dilute even their most criticising remarks and it does not irk the parties concerned, even if what came in print was a scathing attack. Many of them travel to distant lands and are recognised there as geniuses in their own fields of specialisation. Using their magnetic attraction (be it any field they venture into), and physical appearance or their might of pen and spoken word, these people soar to heights hitherto not reached easily by other combinations. The negative effects of 6 & 7 may make them confused and bad-tempered. Such qualities are reflected in their attitudes towards life. Some of them will not find difference between love and lust and find themselves in a quandary, when problems related to personal or private relations arise.

It is interesting to note that the positive effects make these natives of 6 & 7 to become good administrators who understand the problems of the common people. They value the human endeavours and encourage art, literature and science. A couple of them even take up research into notmuchknown fields of science or spiritualism and unearth a new treasure of knowledge useful to mankind. Law or moral values are sometimes overlooked by some of them who are under negative vibrations at one stage or the other. But when the situation demands otherwise, such people do not mind changing their views or practices.

Somehow, this combination of Numbers 6 & 7 has got more number of people who shine easily in the fields where exposure to public is necessary through speech, music, and the written word. (You may conclude that they are matters related rather to mind than to body). But, there are glaring exceptions too. The following list of personalities will enlighten the readers:

★ Newsmakers of 6 & 7:

Lord Ripon

W.H.Wollaston (British Scientist)

Alexandre Dumas (French novelist)

P.G.Wodehouse (English Writer)

Ibn Battuta

BIRTH NUMBER 6 & DESTINY NUMBER 8
(VENUS - SATURN)

The astrological friendliness between Venus and Saturn does not conclude that Number 6 has a lucky Destiny Number in 8. But what the Number 8 lacks, the Birth Number 6 can compensate, although the destiny of 6 & 8 combination leads to subjects like struggles, sacrifices, temples, religion and mysticism. This combination gives more work (both physical and mental) to the people born on the dates of 6. The Number 6 people are basically not "exerting" themselves much and are pleasure-seekers. Thus, the achievements also carry a strain of romanticism and rare techniques which were not hitherto explored by their predecessors.

This combination of 6 & 8 gives many opportunities to the otherwise solitary, philosophical and austere introverts to come into limelight. They become idealists or hard workers (often result-oriented) and earn fame and name. No doubt, they enjoy life although people observing their lives may think that they are not "normal". Generally, the Number 6 & 8 types do not save anything for themselves or for their families. Of course, they know how to earn by using their skill (sometimes, their "skill" may not be acceptable to the society or government). Many take up the causes of others and plunge themselves into an almost unending struggle. Their fame spreads far and wide and the Destiny, in some cases, makes them immune to good advice. That's where the undoing of life begins. It either ruins them fully or makes them resent when it is too late! But, that does not diminish their spirit and they pass away with a satisfaction that they have "done their bit" in the world. They themselves are not aware of the fact that the struggles, the sacrifices and the service they have done for the cause of their people or country will be a monument to be remembered by the posterity. The negative types under this combination are pitied or sympathised with. They become a lesson as to how one should **not** use the "numbers" to satisfy wrong desires or how one should use his numbers for the right purposes.

The Venus - Saturn combine under Numbers 6 & 8 present the under mentioned personalities for the study of readers:

★ **Newsmakers of 6 & 8:**

Lord Kitchener

Marquis de Lafayette

Jean-Paul Marat (French revolution hero)

Thomas De Quincey
(Author of "Confessions of an opium eater")

Capt.de Courcy Bower

126

NUMBER 6 - VENUS

Michelangelo (Painter)

Raphael (Painter)

BIRTH NUMBER 6 & DESTINY NUMBER 9 (VENUS - MARS)

The inverted numerical symbol of 6 will look like 9 and the qualities of Number 6 or Venus also somewhat resemble the reverse of Number 9 or Mars. The general accent of Venus is upon love, affection, friendliness and smooth-sailing attitude whereas Mars lays stress on aggressiveness, war, dynamism and violence. This combination of Venus and mars makes the Number 6 & 9 person a blend of both qualities. The nature, -positive or negative, and the proportion of the blend are the factors that decide the resultant personality.

The blend of positive qualities of both the numbers (planets) causes the 6 & 9 persons to be endowed with a sense of natural justice, fighting for a national cause, despotically benevolent nature, fierce patriotism, interest in the career of a surgeon or a lawyer, willingness to take up any amount of workload and a spirit of adventure. In any field where competition and uncertainty are prevalent, they prove their mettle. If they are poets or writers, they specialise in satires or in lambasting social evils or misrule by the government or vagaries of human behaviour. They prove that "pen is mightier than sword". As artists they choose the subjects which relate to wars, struggles, soul's journey, death, hunting, blood and super-natural events. The film stars and their directors also have a tendency to choose adventures, gunfights, life in uniform and natural catastrophes as their themes. As kings and government heads they always explore the possibility of expanding the area of their influence (sometimes, geographical area also!) The distant galaxies or the Gods and angels provide an interesting vocation or pastime to these people and they prefer to be in the company of such people who talk about them or researching them. The celestial sky, freedom of mind, religion or theosophy.... all these subjects captivate their fertile minds.

The negative types become greedy and covet others' possessions. They do not follow any moral code of life and are law unto themselves. They start a war or make others do it. Their argumentative nature and quarrelsome behaviour irritate others who try to keep off from them. The Birth Number being 6, Venus makes them soft but even then the negative types do not change their attitude. They become adepts in confidence tricks and enjoy life with full vigour and unbridled passion.

Both the types must ensure that their Name Numbers are in harmony with their Birth and/or Destiny Numbers, whichever is lucky and favourable. This is a must for this combination, because the numbers with good or bad vibrations determine if the native is a "positive or negative" type and the world certainly cannot afford to tolerate the negative characters. Such people either kill others and end up in jail or kill themselves, if all the numbers go wrong!

★ **Newsmakers of 6 & 9:**

Velazquez (Spanish Painter)

Sir William Herschel (Astronomer)

Moliere (French dramatist)

Frederick, the great

("Enlightened despot")

Khalil Gibran (Poet)

Ambrose Bierce (American Satirist)

Erwin Rommel (Nazi Field Marshal)

NAME NUMBERS AND THEIR INTERPRETATIONS

If the sum total of the values of letters in your name adds up to 6, then your name number is also said to be under the influence of 6 which represents the planet Venus. The effects of such numbers and their particular characteristics are detailed below:

NUMBER 6 - VENUS

■ **Name No.6:** This number signifies a peaceful life, a satisfied and contented mind and a good standard of living. Being a single digit, it does not have much power.

■ **Name No. 15:** The determination to succeed in all the plans and earn money and the quest for achieving one's ends are signified by this number. Lust, revenge and malice may push the people of this Name number to a vile state of mind. They may become selfish gradually. A charming appearance and forceful speech will help them in achieving their interests. Though this name number is not one conducive to leading a virtuous life, it is one that is ideally suited for purely material success. An alluring personality, excellence in fine arts and a witty nature yield positive results in any activity that can generate huge profits. Many people come forward to help them in need. Life will be luxurious. If their birth number is also favourable, these people will attain fame, wealth and distinction in all aspects of life.

■ **Name No.24:** Those named under this number 24 will receive many favours from the government. This number helps them to reach very high positions in their careers easily. They will marry those who are much higher in status and wealth. If the name number comes under 24, these people can befound progressing very fast in uniformed service like the Defence, Paramilitary forces and the Police. Even if they join as the lowest rank in any field, this number will help them to rise to very high position by its powerful vibrations.

■ **Name No. 33:** This number signifies simultaneous growth in divine grace and prosperity. Those with this name number with or without their knowledge attain spiritual enlightenment surprisingly. Along with divine grace, they are blessed with abundant wealth and properties like granaries, mills etc. They will have many luxurious things at their disposal. They may have everlasting wealth.

129

■ **Name No. 42:** Those named under this number, even if they are poor at the beginning of their lives, will attain a very prominent rank or position in their careers. They may be greedy at times. They will have thrifty bent of mind and are smart in saving money. They hesitate to part with money even for their own comforts in life. Strength of mind and grace will flourish.

■ **Name No.51:** This is the most powerful of all numbers under six. It signifies sudden progress. Those who were just commoners yesterday will become popular and prominent to-day. Unusual circumstances will bring about an unexpected ascent in rank and status. Their body and mind will be bubbling with energy and become uncontrollable. They will be frequently lost in thought, or will become emotionally active and put in untiring efforts in their work. These people who are active in body and mind cannot sleep peacefully. They become restless like a caged lion. To be precise, these people will be ruled by an extra-ordinary energy or power of both body and mind. As there is a possibility of these people making enemies who could threaten their lives, it is advisable for them not to hurt others' sentiments or feelings. This number is considered to be fortunate, as it signifies the accumulation of abundant wealth.

■ **Name No. 60:** This number signifies peace, prosperity, appreciation of fine arts, a balanced state of mind and wisdom. They are skilled conversationalists who can put forth very logical arguments. Their family life will be happy and idealistic. This is quite a fortunate number.

■ **Name No. 69:** The person named under this number will be like an uncrowned king in any business they are involved in. They overtake others and retain their position safely by their own efforts. They are majestic in appearance, very prosperous and will achieve awe-inspiring status. Spurred by emotions, they are known to spend money lavishly for their self-satisfaction. They possess majesty and will lead extremely comfortable and luxurious lives. They are incomparable when it comes to charming others with their tact and speech.

NUMBER 6 - VENUS

■ **Name No.78:** They are the most righteous type among all the Number 6 people. They have a great leaning towards their religion and sometimes follow orthodox beliefs. They can become good poets and can bring the listeners under their spell. They are very generous and are fond of social service. They earn or inherit large sums of money very easily. But, if they are not careful, they could lose all their possessions except the Divine grace. Some of them attain success in occult practice and will be respected by one and all in society.

■ **Name No.87:** This number can give mystic powers. Money will be earned by devious and illegal means. In case of a "negative swing", this number makes people steal at midnight and helps them to charm snakes and tame animals. If birth and destiny numbers are not positive, this number could be related to criminals and bad people. So, the less we discuss, the better.

■ **Name No.96:** This can give a combination of prosperity and higher education. All desires will be fulfilled. They can excel in the fine arts easily. Women will be charmed easily by these people. This is a fortunate number.

■ **Name No.105:** This number can give fortunes, satisfactory environment, great fame and accumulation of wealth. It will beget good progeny.

LOVE AND MARRIAGE

FOR THOSE BORN ON THE 6ᵗʰ, 15ᵗʰ AND 24ᵗʰ OF ANY MONTH

Venus is your planet. You are a natural charmer. You are also easily charmed by the opposite sex. Many things that are beautiful and attractive catch your attention. If you are affected by the "positive" vibrations of Venus, you will be an honest lover or a loyal husband. The "negative" ones become "Philanderers" and are insincere in their relationship. Those among you who are not physically attractive, can still charm the opposite sex with their wealth, status or achievements. Some of you do not think of love or marriage and the mystery is not easy to comprehend!

Your number is 6. Your life partner could be persons born on the 1st, 4th, 5th, 6th or 9th or their series because you would vibrate very well to them and also feel attracted towards them.

For a long term love relation or marriage that you would like to sustain by diplomacy or by adaptability, number 2, 7 or 8 persons are also acceptable.

As far as possible, it is better to avoid 3rd, 12th, 21st and 30th born people.

MISCELLANY

Number 6 persons will find that all the auspicious and important events in their lives are commenced mostly on the 6th, 15th or 24th of any month. Destiny Number 6 also improves their fortunes. 9th, 18th and 27th of every month can also be considered lucky.

3rd, 12th, 21st and 30th of any month and any date having a Destiny Number of 3 are unlucky. Avoid taking important decisions on 5th, 14th and 23rd of any month.

Persons born under the rule of 3 and 6 will extend help; especially, Number 3 persons will help in a big way.

Dark green, blue, any other shades of blue and red are favourable colours. White, Yellow and pink are not recommended.

Lucky gemstone for the Number 6 people is Emerald.

NUMBERS AND NEWS

Anywhere on this earth, snowflakes will always have 6 sides (hexagonal) only. So are the holes in the beehive which, anywhere in the world, have 6 sides. The great architect that is NATURE, designs many beautiful things in terms of 6 only.

Why, the seasons we enjoy are also divided into 6!

NUMBER 7 - NEPTUNE

The most spherical of all the planets of the solar family and almost four times the size of earth is Neptune. It takes more than 13 years to pass through each sign of zodiac and interestingly, perturbs the orbit of its neighbour, Uranus! It revolves quite rapidly on its axis and rules the sign of Pisces.

Neptune, numerologically represented by Number 7, governs mystical aspects of our life, religion, psychism, spiritualism and paranormal happenings. Number 7 people are found in various walks of life but they have always some streak of mystery in them, though they cannot be called "a split personality" one hundred per cent. Revolution and hard work intermingled with intelligence, innovativeness are the bedrock of the character of the positively aspected "Neptunians" or Number 7 people. They have a natural attraction for water, fluids, science, writing, psychic achievements and music. Like other cases, success in their case depends upon a favourable combination of Number 7 with Destiny and Name numbers, though Neptunians are more prone to melancholy to some extent in their lives.

Neptune and Uranus are the prime-movers of the mundane events caused by the all-powerful Destiny. The very word **"Destiny"** implies that there are "unseen, supernatural, cosmological forces" acting on all of us every moment on this earth and they are said to act in a favourable or unfavourable way which makes us fortunate or unfortunate. The planets, Uranus and Neptune are **not** always evil as depicted by some astrologers or occultists.

Their duty is to modify, -each in its own way-the strength of radiation from the SUN and the MOON on the life on earth.

Numerological analysis need not dwell too deeply into the genesis of the theory. So, if readers are aware that URANUS denotes **Number 4** and NEPTUNE denotes **Number 7**, it would suffice.

Number 7 or people born on the 7th, 16th and 25th of any month are ruled by Neptune, the **seer.** The degree to which a man prospers mundanely is determined by Uranus, but Neptune denotes how fit he is or how best he uses his Wisdom, so, Number 7 persons have a **special role** to play on this earth.

The human endeavours are controlled by Number 7 which decides the limits of many things in our lives. 7 days in a week, 7 notes of music, 7 rishis (seers), 7 seas, seven worlds or Paradises, and seven "chakras" in yoga, so on and so forth ....

Positively discussing, the Number 7 people are of philosophic nature. They know where their soul is or where it goes. Intuition, mystic knowledge, prophecy, music (a soul-stirring one!) dreams, poetry, water sports or voyages, religion, histrionics, electronics, yoga and unusual machines and many such things preoccupy their minds and souls. Many excel faster in such fields and become famous and popular. The successful people prove to the world that the other name of luck on this earth is only hard work. They achieve their goals only after struggles, of course, strengthened by their prayers too. They have vivid dreams about an unknown destination, unexplored continent, untried experiment and sometimes an uncertain goal also! In the course of their efforts, they tend to foresee the difficulties or dangers on their routes, but then, it would always be late. There is some kind of melancholy in their process of thought, and some kind of delay in action. Once they plunge themselves, then sky is the limit! So, they must be very careful in studying the pros and cons of any subject before involving themselves in it. This includes all the matters connected to love, affection and matrimony or permanent contracts also.

NUMBER 7 - NEPTUNE

The negative types under Number 7 use God, religion, philosophy, mysticism and human sentiments to exploit the general public to their own advantage. Where the strength of "Karma" (cause & effect phenomenon) is weak, there the negative 7s easily barge in and exploit the gullible. Those people who do ungodly acts in the name of God, those who preach irreligiousness in the name of religion, and those who commit inhuman acts under the cloak of human rights protagonists -invariably have some connection to Number 7 either in their dates of birth, Destiny Numbers, Name Numbers or the Numbers of their names by which they are known in their fields of activity. (Such a surprising relation can be found regarding Karmic planets like Saturn which will be also discussed later).

Please remember, - the world or the society has a greater tendency to be carried away by the "fakes" than by the real ones. With a basic knowledge of Numbers and their cosmological connections, if the readers are able to distinguish between the real and the fake, they will be more and more successful in their lives. You only need to know how harmonious your Numbers are!

Now, having discussed the "mystic" Number 7 and its positive and negative faculties, let us peep into the lives of the interesting persons born under the Birth Number 7 and under various Destiny Numbers.

What the Birth Dates signify

■ Date - 7   This Neptunian date of birth gives intelligence, common sense, discipline, taste in literature or music, skill in fine arts and deep insight into scientific matters. They are patient and hardworking and they attain astounding success in scientific pursuits and literature as well. They may be popular in politics, but are not quite successful in remaining in the top position for a long time due to lack of co-operation of their own friends or due to their inability to sustain their policies. On the other hand, those with a revolutionary approach or with mass appeal survive! Basically, these people are religious and they believe that they are always guided by a superior power. (Even some charlatans among this

135

lot are mistaken by the gullible public as saints!) Willingly or unwillingly, some of them in field of religion happen to act against their conscience and support some public figures with dubious records. That boomerangs later in life. A couple of these persons working hard with their ever-active brains with a quest for ways to improve the world, especially in the field of science, immortalize themselves in history! The people with negative vibrations of this number ruin the world and face a shameful end of their lives.

■ **Date – 16**   If the world needs people with extra-ordinary courage, endurance, versatility and patriotism, such people are mostly found to be born on the 16th, invariably with the support of destiny and name numbers. This date also gives superb talent in music or histrionics and administrative skill, which elevate the persons to high positions in politics. In matters of love, they succeed only if they go the right way. There is some difficulty foreseen in parenting a child. What is outstanding in their lives is a strong mind that helps them to face unexpected challenges. They make good sportsmen or inventors who never get discouraged by any pitfalls they come across. On the other hand, they forge ahead with renewed vigour. They have a unique way of solving the day-to-day problems, especially in politics or statecraft and would never waver from their decisions once taken, whether their followers or colleagues approve of it or not! Interestingly, in spite of their steadfast attitude, they make very good negotiators in times of crisis and persuade people or nations to accept their suggestions or ideas. If there are some mystics or people of religion under this category, they should guard themselves against uttering anything in public that may be controversial.

■ **Date – 25**   This date of birth belongs to highly opinionated people and those who think originally and act originally. They have a novel way of giving a message without minding the criticism or admiration it may invite. Their words and actions, whether they are kings or subjects, may cause a flutter in the least or a revolution at the most. But it is bound to influence the course of history! Lucky are those among them who survive the aftermath. Others perish tragically or go into oblivion. They are people who do not work as a team but strive hard as a single person to achieve some remarkable goal as in the case of scientists, artists and writers. Their contribution to the world will be praiseworthy. A good number of these people are respected in countries other than their own and some of them even choose to live there permanently. A few of those born on 25th invent some strange doctrines and try to propagate them, but fail miserably for the simple reason that those doctrines are misconstrued only to instigate violence, though it must have servd their purpose initially. Generally, with very few exceptions, this date brings in respect, authority and honour. (It is not known why the Presidents of India are sworn in mostly on the 25th July every time. Is it considered so auspicious...?)

People born under Birth Number 7 (7th, 16th and 25th of any month) and with various Destiny Numbers will find their lives as follows:

BIRTH NUMBER 7 & DESTINY NUMBER 1 (NEPTUNE -SUN)

The basic faculties that come with Number 7 indicate the personality and skills of the person and how best they are used or what the result of such action will be, are determined by Number 1.

Humour, Media, Poetry, Philosophy, Religion, Music, Metaphysics, Scientific pursuits to help humanity in every-day-life, ... and subjects related to Neptune as related in the introduction to Number 7, are the ideal fields for the 7 & 1 characters. Since the Destiny Number 1 somewhat modifies the effect of Number 7 or influencing it in such a way that the natives get a leading or governing position in their respective fields, they become indispensable in any field they are placed. Their unique style of functioning distinguishes them from the others. They have a rebellious nature but that is in the interest of giving the world a gift of rare nature or something which the world had never seen or heard before. In philosophy or religion they take sides and do not compromise with any theory which does not suit their taste. Or else, they rather prefer to remain agnostics!

However, intuition or a rare instinct does rule them and in all their actions it is manifested. That is why, in any field of activities, they prefer to exhibit their own skill, talents or performance as of superior quality. They hardly bother about what others think. If anyone connected to them mistakes them for egoists, then he will be proved wrong! With proper Name Numbers and harmonious numbers of the team members (may be formed naturally or by choice), the 7 & 1 persons achieve better than other combinations under this series.

The negative types under this series suffer a lot. They earn their own followers and their own enemies too. Unlike the positive types under Number 7 & 1 combination, the negative ones become slaves of their strange habits and behaviour. They face law suits, quarrels, humiliation and are despised by the state and the society. When they die, the whole world does not realise that there were scholars amidst us, though eclipsed by scandals. But it would be always too late! That is why it is necessary for these people to be in good company and with good morals. Numerological research has proved that even if these negative types knock at the door of a well-meaning, sympathizing and able Numerologist, they can remedy their faults and resurrect their future.

★ **Newsmakers of 7 & 1 :**

Queen Elizabeth I

Lord Beaverbrook (British Press Baron)

Charlie Chaplin (Comedian of great renown)

W.Somerset Maugham

Noel Coward

Sean Connery

David Copperfield

NUMBER 7 - NEPTUNE
BIRTH NUMBER 7 & DESTINY NUMBER 2 [NEPTUNE - MOON]

Both the numbers, 7 and 2 are related to the active mind from which emanate philosophy, mysticism, poesy, meditation or yogic practices and intense feelings of patriotism or spirit of unusual (and even unexpected) achievement. **Neptune**, (significator of emotional Wisdom) and **Moon**, (significator of thought or mind) are said to be in good harmony under this combination, though variations are not ruled out due to Name Numbers and allied factors.

The 7 & 2 characters mostly are found in the fields connected to contemplation, power of imagination and the skills related to controlling body and mind. Their vivid imagination helps them to become great poets or writers of excellent verses or essays. What is basically different in their works is their originality. Their power of learning or mastering a language is phenomenal. They observe people and places and honestly record what they see and experience. Inclined towards religion and mysticism, they have a liberal outlook regarding such matters as God, religion or scriptures, which makes them "universal personalities"! Some of them will have always a group of people following them. It is not necessary that the said group must consist of only the disciples, fans or followers. It may consist of people who would one day betray, criticize, or even turn enemies! So, care and caution must be exercised. Whatever may be their profession, these people exhibit their talents in their own fields and are generally accepted without any reservations. Occult sciences or occult power comes to them easily but many of them (as per the research data available) do not practice it as profession. They are epoch-makers in the fields of writing, painting, music and sports and express their ideas with freedom. In other fields, they find a lot of restrictions and sometimes, they even become victims of their own opinions or performance.

Under this combination of 7 & 2, even the negative types, if any found, seem to play "soft-pedaling" in their behaviour -probably, they may

139

feel that "the human minds" are too delicate to hurt. Of course, changing opinions, places, friends or jobs is not uncommon among these people. The "practical" types who choose their career in public life might become victims of their own pragmatic approach.

Some notable personalities given here below will help the readers to probe more and more into this combination of No. 7 & 2.

★ **Newsmakers of 7 & 2:**

Mark Chagall (Painter)

Mohammed Anwar El Sadat (Egyptian President)

Madonna (Pop Singer)

Dwight Gooden

Pullela Gopichand

BIRTH NUMBER 7 & DESTINY NUMBER 3 (NEPTUNE – JUPITER)

There is a peculiarity with Number 3 which represents Jupiter. It makes its natives to work harder, if it comes as a Destiny Number. The hard-working natives would do sacrifices readily in one form or the other but not all the others. The Number 7 people are basically a "thinking type" and if Number 3 as a Destiny Number makes them work harder physically, the combination may cause sufferings to the person, but not always! There is some amount of luck connected to this combination, because like a few other combinations the 7 & 3 types do not miss the fruits of their labour. They are rather successful as writers, publishers, travel managers or advertisers, than in any other professions. Research into strange subjects and one form of the art or the other offers them successful venues. If the Name Numbers are lucky, the efforts of Number 7 & 3 persons are admired and duly rewarded. Otherwise, this combination leaves the people working hard and sacrificing the benefits all along their lives .**The lives of such people with disharmonious name numbers may not be eventful and they may not come into limelight.**

There are negative vibrations in some specific cases which make these people marry more than once or change their loyalty often in love affairs. It does not mean that they are immoral.

They are "choosy" in their friendships or love, because Number 3 as Destiny Number gives them a habit of viewing life as an idealist. They are hardly satisfied with the environs, the colleagues, the jobs they do or the hobbies they pursue. They are good citizens without fixity of their goals and they depend upon one form of prayer or worship or the other to enlighten themselves about their future. Sometimes, their courage or obstinacy may reach its extremes and they tend to be foolhardy. At such moments they gamble with the opportunities available. In many cases, their prayers are heard and they achieve their goals. They are a healthy blend of ancient and modern values and their love of nature, art, and more especially their devotion to duty will earn a good name for them. As such, they must bear with all the sacrifices they initially do and understand that "there will be a bright light at the end of the tunnel!"

★ **Newsmakers of 7 & 3:**

Sir Edwin Landseer (English Painter of fame)

Charles Dickens (Famous author)

Jane Austen

Naushad

Pope Benedict XVI

BIRTH NUMBER 7 & DESTINY NUMBER 4 (NEPTUNE-URANUS)

In occult texts these two numbers, 7 and 4 are said to be "friendly" to each other, but as a Destiny Number, 4 has the habit of directing some negative vibrations towards those born on anyone of the dates of 7 series. The natives under No. 7 & 4 combination may have sudden changes in their plans or destiny causes sudden incidents which drastically affect the lives of 7 & 4 people. It may be of positive results or negative which again depends upon the Name Numbers and the dates of activities.

The basic nature of Number 7 is to be "different" from others. Each person under Number 7 has a new message to the world. He may be a scientist, sports person, philosopher, mystic or a politician. The 7 -series people in general, are intuitive, imaginative and god-fearing. Their inward compassion for the suffering humanity will not be easily visible outside and when Number 4 comes as Destiny Number, the 7 & 4 persons seem to be hard-hearted and selfish.

Those who are close to them would tell that the fact is otherwise. The over-involvement of Number 7 will be countered by Number 4 as the Destiny Number. At the same time the stubbornness and the strict sense of discipline due to the influence of Number 4, earns a bad name for the Number 7 people. If the Destiny Number 4 causes negative vibrations, the 7 & 4 person becomes the most feared one. On the other hand, 7 & 4 helps a person to achieve all their noble goals and they become trend-setters in whichever field they enter.

There are some "malefic" vibrations caused by the "naturally malefic" combination of planets which, in most of the cases, affect only the personal lives of the Number 7 & 4 people. When they are at the peak of their performance or achievement, some unexpected "change" takes place which retards the progress made by them. Those who have good and harmonious Name Numbers are found to overcome this problem also, though the mystery of such happening is not quite apprehensible.

If you dwell deeply into the wonderful lives of the following 7 & 4 personalities, you may stumble into the answer:

★ Newsmakers of 7 & 4:
Madame Marie Curie
Guglielmo Marconi
Sir Francis Galton
Lee Kuan Yew
Ben-Gurion (The first P.M. of Israel)
Mihir Sen
Russell Crowe

BIRTH NUMBER 7 & DESTINY NUMBER 5
[NEPTUNE- MERCURY]

The basically intuitive, imaginative and investigative types under Number 7 are influenced to a great extent by the versatile, fast and resourceful Number 5. If constructively influenced, they are instrumental in bringing peace and harmony to the world. If otherwise, they become the cause of anarchy, bloodshed and destruction. Interestingly, they, - positive or negative in their vibrations, do leave indelible images in the history.

Generally, the Number 7 types carry a strain of melancholy, in their personality. They love solitude, peaceful meditation, lonely contemplation, investigative research, philosophy of some specific religion, group or science and shine in all pursuits connected to the aforesaid subjects. Number 5, when it appears as Destiny Number, brings some positive changes in Number 7's personality. It brings in an element of versatility and attachment to the mundane world. Thus, the combination becomes a very good blend which is useful to the society at large. It makes them venture in so many fields and makes them talented in more than one art or science. The inquisitiveness of Number 7 mixed with the industriousness or dynamism of Number 5 produces one of the most respected personalities on this earth. Such people endeavour hard to help the humanity live in comfort, happiness and harmony. They educate or entertain the people. Their inventions and discoveries and their loyalty to the cause they espouse kindles awe and respect in all spheres of human life. Their lives or deaths always evoke a sense of learning to the observers. When the positive or constructive types become legends in the history of the world, the negative types also become so, but their admirers are a small group consisting of ignorant or innocent followers. The latter group suffers even without knowing the cause of their suffering!

There are some peculiar traits with this combination. When they gamble with their mundane dice, they need to be careful, especially in politics, statecraft or society. The initial success takes them too far in imagining the results, even though such results may be found later, "bitter pills to swallow" or intangible. But, this particular group of 7 & 5 combination forges ahead and of course, achieves the goal **at any cost!** This is where Fate and Freewill head towards the same direction.

The readers who want to know more about the Number 7 & 5 combination may go through deeply the lives of the following people:

★ **Newsmakers of 7 & 5:**

Gregory Rasputin

Archibald Philip Primrose of Rosebery

Ronald Amundsen (Antarctic explorer)

Lord Louis Mountbatten (The last viceroy of India)

Sir Isaac Newton

Ravi Shankar (Sitarist)

BIRTH NUMBER 7 & DESTINY NUMBER 6 [NEPTUNE - VENUS]

Though almost all Number 7s are thinkers, writers, or philosophers, when Number 6 comes into their lives as Destiny Number, they play some "special" notes. They bring in some kind of reform with the help of their pursuits. Not all appreciate it. Some feel that the "reform" has violated a legal provision or an accepted practice. Some others feel that the attempt to introduce such a "reform" is preposterous. If such a "reform" is introduced in the field of politics, it is again supposed to cause a flutter. However, despite the initial hesitation (or you may call it suspicion) or disbelief, if the 7 & 6 person declares that he has invented or discovered or introduced something **new** in the field of science, it is accepted! Lucky scientists that they are!

The vibrations of Neptune and Venus are mutually friendly as viewed by astrological observers. But when the Birth Number is 7, the Destiny Number of Venus, viz., 6 does not confer its favourable results. Though the qualities of Venus (Number 6) are manifest on a Number 7 personality, the benefits are not fully conferred. The hesitation prolonged contemplation, lack of trust, hasty or fool-hardy actions, and undue dependence or public support cause a great damage to the person's plans. As such, there is no room for any contingency in their planning. So, unexpected problems and opposition crop up and it mostly affects the domestic life also. In the bargain, Number 7 & 6 person is badly battered by Destiny and in most of the cases, the ultimate loss is difficult to swallow. But there is a Solace! The abnormal mental faculties of Number 7 are always ready to face any eventuality and the person will survive the onslaught of time. What more, Number 6 (Venus) is standing by to cheer up and pep up! However, if these people check up their Name Numbers, there may be ways to remedy the malady. If not, the pages of history always await them!

The combination of Numbers 7 & 6 provides a list of interesting personalities in its category. Browse the list and find out the reasons as to why some are successful and why some others are not!

★ **Newsmakers of 7 & 6:**

Ralph Waldo Emerson (American essayist)

Sir James Young Simpson
(Scottish obstetrician)

Archbishop William Laud
(Archbishop of Canterbury)

Wilbur Wright
(Co-inventor of of Airplane)

James Madison
(4th American President)

Robert Browning
(Victorian poet of England)

John McEnroe
(American Tennis Player)

MY FORTUNE

BIRTH NUMBER 7 & DESTINY NUMBER 7
(NEPTUNE-NEPTUNE)

This is a combination of Numbers that call for rare feats in life. It has a shroud of mystery. The people signified by it like solitude or independence of thought, word and action. Many of them are lone performers. Only when their actions are declared openly, the world would brace up and say, "Wow! That was it!" It is important that this combination should be positive, because the negative characters go to any extent to harm others' interests. Since both the Birth and Destiny Numbers are one and the same, they should never take an extreme position in any issue or crisis. Policy of moderation in case of any crisis helps them. Many of them who are outwardly men of logic (about the subjects of religion, god and super-natural events) are inwardly believers in the celestial powers that control us. They research into any subject on hand and become convinced of the facts within. Then only they speak out. This nature of silent analysis makes them mystics, scientists, and lone pursuers of one form of art or the other. With somewhat negative vibrations, they become good "spies" or, to speak of extremes, - those "who suspect everyone around"! They are nature lovers and good environs, forests, hills, waterfalls or any place of scenic beauty attracts them. Their independent nature is appreciated by those who watch them in action.

Interestingly, even if the Number 7 & 7 formulates a policy or a methodology, it is not disputed or disagreed with for a long time to come. On the other hand, when such an opinion is improved to suit the changing times, the lustre is lost. However, if they contemplate deeply, work relentlessly and discover something unheard of earlier, such beliefs and doctrines formed on the rockbed of logic (not on emotions!) become great expressions of human thought or philosophy. Because of such qualities, the 7 & 7 types are capable of changing the very face or function of their society, country, or the world. Such people, though they may be disbelievers in the omnipotence of fate, find themselves helpless when fate overtakes their freewill one day in their lives!

However, their exploits or experiences become lessons to many people all over the world and inspire them to work harder. They leave a legacy to the world in which they lived and when they die, they are not forgotten (even the "negative" ones too!).

If the "sevens" visit the heavens, they revolutionise the system there also! Learn more about the 7 & 7 characters given below and search for more examples in the contemporary period:

★ **Newsmakers of 7 & 7:**

Lu Xun
(Chinese poet)
John Foster Dulles
(U.S. Secretary of State)
Sir. C.V.Raman
(Indian Physicist - Nobel Laureate)
Norman Borlaug
(Father of "Green revolution.")
Conrad Hilton
(Hotelier)
Vladimir Putin (Russian President)

BIRTH NUMBER 7 & DESTINY NUMBER 8
(NEPTUNE - SATURN)

The intuitive knowledge-seeker or the philosopher who judges even the minute details of any issue and works hard to put his thoughts into action could be **none other than Number 7 & 8** person.

Under conflicting vibrations, they would become very reserved (sometimes introverts also!) and act cynically or tactlessly underestimating the odds of life. They may be betrayed by friends and find themselves at loggerheads with the law or the general public or their spouses!

MY FORTUNE

From whatever standpoint you view the people under 7 & 8 combination, you would finally say "They need not have done like this! ... It should not have been their fate". Don't expect them to care for your advice, if any, you could give. They won't heed! They are not fat-headed or bad tempered egoists, but on the other hand, they are capable of achieving their goals. They have noble ideals but in making others follow them, the 7 & 8 personalities become hasty. The strong "karmic influence" causes a lot of mishaps in their career and personal lives. The pity is that in spite of their sharp intellect, they fail to judge their partners or friends. They find that at one moment or the other, the less intelligent or the not-so-efficient ones overtake them and win the race of life. Such winners also know very well that, being minnows, they have won against the titans. Summing up all the narratives, we must say that only such of the 7 & 8 personalities win and retain their success, who understand, analyse and act according to the "psyche" of their followers, family members or colleagues. Others perish in the struggle!

The personal lives of the 7 & 8 persons are generally not very much attended to. There is always some deficiency or difficulty with which most of the 7 & 8 people live. Religion, politics and the suffering masses pre-occupy the minds of those born under this combination and the personal well-being is given the go-by! Well, as Frost said, "They have promises to keep and miles to go before they sleep!". In fields like art, music, sculpture and statesmanship, they popularise their own brand or product, which, later becomes the hallmark! Interestingly, the planet of TIME, Saturn, -though causing its vibrations on the natives of 7 & 8 because of its association, does not confer what is called LUCK. But, the Name Numbers if planned correctly or exist correctly by themselves (as could be seen in the lives of the successful 7 & 6), will play a prominent and favourable role in their lives. Such people fight the odds and win the game of life with flying colours. (Please note that the Name Numbers must be studied before they plunge into matrimony!).

NUMBER 7 - NEPTUNE

Dig out as many 7 & 8 personalities like those given below from the pages of human history. You will come to know that Numerology has a treasure of knowledge about integers and individuals.

★ **Newsmakers of 7 & 8:**

Oliver Cromwell

(Lord Protector of the commonwealth)

William Wordsworth

(English romantic poet)

Sir Austen Chamberlain

(British statesman who got Nobel Prize.)

Thomas Macaulay

(British Historian)

Oscar Wilde

(Irish Writer & poet)

Ivan Lendl

(Tennis Champion)

Pablo Picasso

(Modern artist of Spanish Origin)

BIRTH NUMBER 7 & DESTINY NUMBER 9 (NEPTUNE - MARS)

The combination of 7 & 9 has not been discussed in all its fullness by many of the practitioners so far. In most of the books (there are only very few discussing the relations exclusively between Birth and Destiny Numbers) or theatres of professional discussions, the really serious combination of the Numbers 7 and 9, has not been taken even for a casual analysis. A few who have ventured to write have "welcomed" the combination, stating that the contemplative, philosophical and dignified 7 will become positively activated by the tenacious, authoritative and capable 9. I beg to differ from this view and in the light of a horde of evidences collected regarding popular personalities and on the basis of my experience, I am compelled to tell a different tale!

149

Number 7 persons are people of sharp intellect, researching brain and of intuition. But, when they stumble into truth, they come out of their "shells" and try to herald the news eloquently. When Number 9 (or Mars) comes as Destiny Number, the Number 7 people can hardly restrain themselves and they make their point vehemently or act forcefully! Suddenly, the "martial" nature takes the lead in their personality. They are impelled by the red, aggressive, warrior-like Planet of War. Force, courage and strength, hitherto not seen in the personality of Number 7 person, predominates him and **"Mr. Seven"** is ready for action! The pity is that emotions and personal considerations overcome reason and practicality, thus something drastic takes place in the life or career or the 7 & 9 persons. Blood, weapons, destruction and anarchy on one extreme (when Mars is exalted and afflicted) and arguments, quarrels, law suits or hatred on the other extreme are the common features of **negatively associated Mars.**

There is no need to fear this combination because the planet Mars represented by Number 9 can give mental (and physical) strength, ambition, leadership qualities, endurance, willingness to take responsibilities, logic and an enjoyable company. This is possible in two ways. The Name Number **must be harmonious** or the negative vibrations of Mars must be under control or nil! Only a qualified, experienced and an enlightened Numerologist can find it out. Quacks and imposters will cause a greater harm! Beware!

The people with 9 as Destiny Number though their Birth Numbers are "soft" or "passive" ones, have proved to the world that Mars (or Number 9) has only added to their mental strength and endurance in their valuable service to mankind, e.g. Mahatma Gandhi, Dr.Rukmani Arundale, Albert schweitzer and many more. This is the positive side of Number 9 or Mars.

The positive types with good Name Numbers become popular with their skill of music, interpretation of religious scriptures, mystic sciences or occultism, metaphysical phenomenon and even materialism. Their arguments, though forcible, are very appealing to the senses and people long to hear them again. Their humour is harmless and their purpose is blemishless. Their speeches or performances are feast to the eyes and ears of the posterity. Generally, they pay less attention to their family life, because of their pride that they have a more "meaningful" mission in their lives. The significator of Wisdom **Neptune** and the significator of the martial spirit **Mars** give these "positive" natives both Wisdom and Force that emancipates the masses from their ignorance.

★ **Newsmakers of 7 & 9:**

Sir Joshua Reynolds

(A great English Painter of the 18th Century)

H.M.Muzaffar-Al-Din

(Shah of Persia who died in exile in 1907)

Virginia Woolf (Feminist Lady novelist; committed suicide)

William Colgate (Founder of Soap & Toothpaste Empire)

James R. Birle (American Businessmen)

(The readers are welcome to send correct details about any popular person with No. 7 & 9 combination in their community or country which will help the ongoing research.)

NAME NUMBERS AND THEIR INTERPRETATIONS

Now let us look into the qualities of those having various name numbers under Number 7 ruled by Neptune.

■ **Name No.7:** This name number represents high principles and virtuous qualities, which may flourish with divine grace. Unexpected changes will take place. Efforts will not produce the desired results.

■ **Name No.16:** This number signifies speedy progress and a sudden downfall. Ancient texts depict this number by a picture showing the shattering of a tall tower and a king's head with his crown falling from its top. This truth was proved when Japan (16) fell prey to the nuclear bombs. The Japanese Emperor was considered to be God-incarnate and his people would not even look at him from an elevated place. Unfortunately, the Americans bombed Japan stripping the Emperor of his status and the consequences are well known even today. If your name number is 16, it is better to change it to some other lucky number. This number induces new imaginative thoughts which will be reflected in the writings of the person.

■ **Name No.25:** As this number gives good results in the end, it can be considered a good number. These people will undergo many trials in life. Every step in life will present problems and difficulties. The victory gained over such problems will give them self-confidence, spiritual growth and the support of those around them. They are worldly-wise, known for clarity of thought and hence their actions will be well-planned. These people will establish ideals and standards for themselves and will adhere to them at all costs. Just as gold when cleansed of all impurities becomes shiny and precious, the lives of these people will end with respect and honour after many trials. (Note the life of Mahatma Gandhi who used to sign as M.K.Gandhi).

Note: The illustrations and notes that I offer for the numbers enumerated in this book are from ancient texts which are more than a thousand years old. It is for the convenience of the readers I wanted to provide examples citing some recent personalities and it should not be concluded that this research is based on recent incidents and persons. Facts contained in this book apply very well even to the contemporary personalities and recent incidents. Examples are given only to elucidate those attributes that are mentioned in this book.

■ **Name No.34:** In a way, this number can also be called lucky. This number will openly display the best qualities and capabilities of these persons in an attractive manner. It improves their stature but cannot be considered as fortunate. If the birth number is also a favourable one, they can earn enormous wealth quite easily. If not, earning money itself will become a problem. **There will be some problem in their family life. Most of the men will either be addicted to women or wine.** Their minds easily succumb to sensuous pleasures. This is the most fearful aspect of this number. (Be cautious about it)! Hence, they are advised to change this Name number to a more fortunate one.

■ Name No.43: This is a strange number. Their whole life will be revolutionary. Whatever profession in which they are involved, this number produces new enemies. They have the tendency to resign from their jobs often. They will be constantly bringing out extreme ideas. They have extraordinary powers of imagination, speaking and writing as in the case of the other name numbers under 7. Their desires will be fulfilled at the end. This number, which is regarded as somewhat unlucky, indicates trials, great obstacles and revolutionary changes. They are sure to succeed in their ideals. (It is unlucky in the sense that they do not enjoy the luxuries or comforts of a peaceful life. Even their success will not yield them any personal gains). Their shrewdness increases with age, but they will encounter more criticism than praise for their capabilities and intelligence.

■ Name No. 52: This number also signifies some type of revolutionary qualities. If the birth number is favourable it could bring world renown. They readily offer a solution to any problem and can charm many. If they are on the spiritual path, they can attain great powers and immense popularity. All their desires will be fulfilled. **They can bring about a new era in the lives of others.** (This power can also be found in number 25 to a certain extent). Their end will come abruptly, leaving their work unaccomplished. Although their personal life will be fraught with problems, they are sure to be famous and favoured by all.

■ Name No.61: These people will quit a comfortable life and try new avenues according to their wishes. Successes and failures come in succession. If they can take care of their health, their later years will be

153

quite fruitful helping them win prestigious posts. Though they may seem to be leading happy lives, in reality, they will be unhappy in their family lives. They spend much time in making new efforts and will achieve victory. They will earn great fame.

■ **Name No.70:** People represented by this number are of extreme nature. Their comfortable life gets disturbed by circumstances. There are frequent disappointments, failures and problems. But the later years will be fruitful, successful and filled with blessings. This number does not possess much power. If their destiny number is favourable, these people will be happy during their final years. If not, their problems may drown them in misery.

■ **Name No. 79:** People of this number tend to suffer very badly in the beginning of their lives due to many difficulties. Later, these people will rise quickly by their cleverness and sheer will power. They will settle down very comfortably and will succeed in their endeavours. They will have popular support, a comfortable life and will achieve enduring success. They become very fortunate with the passage of time and also become great personalities.

■ **Name No. 88:** This number gives spiritual progress. They are generous and compassionate. They are affectionate to all creatures and will become popular.

■ **Name No.97:** This number gives proficiency in the scriptures and fine arts. It also gives eminence in spiritual career. They will be successful in all their efforts and will be prosperous due to their astounding achievements in chosen fields.

■ **Name No. 106:** There will be drastic changes in life. They will experience many problems during their middle age. Their later years will be comfortable. They get into big troubles that cannot be solved easily. This number is not a lucky one. Greed for worldly things will supercede the interest in seeking divine grace.

NUMBER 7 - NEPTUNE

LOVE AND MARRIAGE

FOR THOSE BORN ON THE 7th, 16th AND 25th OF ANY MONTH

Neptune is your planet. It is a rapidly revolving planet and has a strange habit of perturbing the orbit of its neighbour, Uranus! This also has the power of affecting the events on this earth, especially when they are related to politics, fine arts or science, or super-natural happenings. People who are represented by the planet Neptune, have acute sense of probing into human minds and subjects hitherto unknown. As for love and marriage, these people's lives become a sort of experiment. Lucky are those who have a harmonious and prosperous married life. Research reveals that such people have strong and harmonious name numbers and destiny numbers!

Your Number is 7. The Neptunian vibrations are found favourable to numbers 2, 4 and 6 and so the people born on those dates and their series are found attractive. Marriage or long term love life will be fine.

If name numbers and destiny numbers are harmonious, even those born on the 3rd, 4th, 5th,7th and 9th and their series of dates will be found friendly and satisfied with their relations with Number 7 people.

However, Number 8 persons are not suitable for long term relations or for marriage. Marriage with Number 1 persons is not conducive for progeny, and generally it is considered antipathic.

The general rule for Number 7 people is that they must go in for long term love or marriage only when the name numbers and Birth numbers of the persons concerned are harmonious.

MISCELLANY

Lucky dates for the people born on the 7th, 16th and 25th of any month are 2nd, 11th, 20th and 29th. They become successful even if Number 2 comes as the Destiny Number of the said dates. 25th also is a fortunate one. Choosing the 1st, 10th, 19th or 28th is also good. However, the factors like Name Number and Destiny Number are also to be taken

155

into account while choosing 29th and 28th of any month.

Dates 7, 16, 8, 17, 26 are to be avoided. Even Destiny Numbers of 7 or 8 are unlucky.

To those born under Number 7 dates, Numbers 1, 2, and 4 will extend help, when needed.

White, Pale yellow, Light green or Light blue are fortunate colours. All dark colours like red and black should be avoided.

Regarding lucky gemstones, cat's eye or pearls will make them prosperous in career or marriage.

NUMBERS AND NEWS

Number 7 stands for the expression of the mysterious God force in nature in all religions.

The seven Devis of Hindus, the seven Amschaspands of Parsees, the seven Archangels of Revelation, the seven Sephiroth of the Hebrew kabbalah, ... and so on.

In the material world too, we have seven days a week, seven basic shades of light, seven continents, seven seas, seven basic races of human beings, seven layers of atmosphere ... it goes on in divisions of seven.

In occult philosophy the power of Number seven is fully understood. 7 is the only number capable of dividing 'the number of eternity' i.e. 1 and 0 placed by its side - as many times as you want. Say,

1,000,000 ÷ 7 = 142857

You will Repeatedly get only the repetitions of the same 142857

(By natural addition you also get the root number 9, the final single digit!)

Respect Number 7; it will show you the Heaven!

NUMBER 8 - SATURN

There are planets that are *natural benefics* which confer good results and there are planets which confer bad results and are called *natural malefics*. The human beings who, throughout their lives may be good and noble-hearted, but circumstances or **Karma** make them "bad" at times. It is possible that even those who are bad and of despicable nature **sometimes** exhibit very good qualities and do such things that are always remembered by the mankind with gratitude. That is why the ancient seers of India, who, even without any **known** scientific instruments observed the planets' movements in space and concluded that there are no hard and fast rules that make the benefic and malefic qualities of planets permanent. It is possible that a naturally malefic planet could become a *functional benefic* and naturally benefic planet may become a *functional malefic*. Astrologically speaking, the resultant behaviour of **any** planet in a horoscope depends upon the sign of the zodiac it occupies, its aspects on various planets and houses, other planets' aspects or influence on it and many other factors, such as, transits in the celestial sky etc. Numerology also follows some such rules that are simpler in nature and applications. The planet in discussion - SATURN which is a natural malefic and also the most dreaded one (!), has interesting stories to tell in the pages to come!

Saturn, the **"ringed wonder"** of the celestial sky is a slow-moving planet. It takes two years and a half to complete its journey through each sign of Zodiac. The fact that it is the chief significator of one's KARMA (the cause and effect phenomenon) is evidently understood by us when we come across certain situations in our lives, which prove to be agonising physically or mentally -for reasons unknown! Justice, in its real sense, is its motto and in rendering the same Saturn shows no fear or favour. That is why it is considered the **"celestial judge"** and it has chosen Libra ------ "a pair of scales", as its sign of exaltation. Hence, Number 8 that represents Saturn rules all those born on the dates of 8 primarily, such as 8th, 17th and 26th of any month and also those whose Destiny Number is 8.

Of all the numbers that we discuss under the subject of Numerology, Number 8 that represents SATURN has a unique place. The persons under the Birth or Destiny Number of 8 are meant for hard work, either physically or mentally. You will find many Number 8 people among us who work hard to achieve their goals, but you may not easily recognise them, because such hard workers could be under any other combinations such as, Number 3, Number 1 or Number 9 and the like. When all the other "hard workers" take it easy in the event of failure or opposition, the 8s "take it to their hearts". There is always a streak of melancholy in their character and destiny. The positive ones work hard for the progress of their society or country and are worshipped in their own spheres of influence. But, by a quirk of "fate" some problem arises and they meet with disappointment, failure, dissatisfaction or derailment of plans. The mission is cut short and they lose their peace of mind, their position, friends or money or sometimes, even their lives when the "negative" 8 reacts violently. On the other hand, the positive "8" makes the people around share his or her misery and the latter puts up with the situation patiently. This is because of the philosophic bent of mind that gives the "positive" 8s an abnormal sense of duty and purpose of action. At times, the world mistakes them for "escapists" but sooner or later it comes to know that they are "crouching tigers" biding their time only to "pounce at the right moment and kill"!

One of the peculiarities of the Number 8 people is that even with the **luckiest** Destiny Number, they cannot enjoy their lives as others do. The darker side of the world arouses curiosity in them. Mysteries of the universe, metaphysics, paranormal events, secret sexual behaviour of people, crime-related stories or news, occultism, espionage, inventions or discoveries which involve denouncing a time-honoured theory and extreme views or actions warranting the wrath of others are Number 8 people's interests! In brief, they are either unconventional or very orthodox.

However, the Name Numbers do have a role to play in their lives. The bad vibrations can be nullified and success and peace can be achieved if harmonious Name Numbers are selected for the Number 8 people. Good Name Numbers can even modify their character and outlook favourably. Thus, Number 8 people who are ruled by Saturn can counter the negative vibrations with the help of good Destiny Numbers and harmonious Name Numbers. The readers will come to know in the following chapters how Numerology has provided a remedy to any malady as far as Number 8 people under various Destiny Numbers are concerned!

What the Birth Dates signify

■ Date - 8 This Saturnian date of birth influences people to a great extent during the process of upbringing. They learn quite early in life that achievements are possible only by synchronizing mind and body while at work. Soldiers, sportsmen and politicians reach the top positions by exerting themselves, though people born under other combinations do not put in as much effort. Those born on the 8th and are in the race for a throne or top most rank in the military or politics, have to always face a risk element. Some may face their ends in a tragic manner. Goddess of Luck, however, smiles upon those who are inventors, administrators, and literateurs whose intellect and hard work are duly rewarded. A couple of them even get international recognition. Many people who belong to the field of religion, achieve worldwide fame and breathe their last with a satisfaction that their message is heard and relished. They are adored even by the people of various other faiths. Foreseeing difficulties in career well before time or watching for signs of ill-health, will keep them in good stead. Temptation for unnatural sensual pleasures overtakes some of them who easily fall prey to them. They may have to sacrifice their progress or peace of mind. This is because of negative name numbers which should be avoided. Spiritual pursuits or social reforms give them some relief.

MY FORTUNE

■ **Date – 17** This is one of the interesting dates of birth. Those born on this date struggle hard to be rich or to be in the limelight and achieve what they want after overcoming all the challenges. There is always some degree of secrecy or mystery shrouding their physical ailments or mental turmoils. Yet, they learn to present a rosy picture of their lives to others. Their versatility and ability to reach for the sky will be most probably known only in the latter half of their lifetime. Only then, the world does come to know that these people's merits were recognized so late. Many of them become outstanding sports persons and writers of classics. This is one date of birth on which a couple of religious heads are born although agnostics or rationalists are commonly found under this category! However, they become popular and create history. The date of birth 17 shows the way to success. Sometimes it may be a phenomenal success in politics, and it is necessary for those born on this date to seize the opportunity, when Goddess Luck knocks at their door. Physical fitness or mental agility is part of their personality and those who belong to the filmdom or art world live longer and satisfactorily healthier. Some of them shine very well on a foreign soil and they make history. The negative vibrations of destiny number or name number prove to be harmful and may lead to miserable ends.

■ **Date – 26** One of the numbers that constitute a date of birth on which both good and bad were born is 26! Curiously enough, they shoot to fame, power and wealth irrespective of their conduct or principles. Difficult childhood, loss of a parent, disturbed education or profession, frequent changes of residence, immigrating to distant or foreign countries and researching habit are the points foreseen in their lives. Such things affect both the good and the bad born on the 26th and of course, the degree of experience varies from person to person. On the positive side, they possess an extra-ordinary will power (in some cases spiritual power) and single-minded devotion to whatever vocation they choose. **They excel all others in an unprecedented way.** They turn pebbles into diamonds and rubbles into skyscrapers. Those who are in the fields of religion, literature, theatre or social service become legends during their lifetime itself and are ever idolized thereafter. The scientists and inventors overcome several challenges, and achieve their goals, while those who belong to other numbers pull out from the race or perish. The world would appreciate their stoicism and courage which may be incomparable in history. But there is always a danger lurking to the life and efforts of the people in politics or in power. Some of them are very badly battered and even punished for wrong decision which they have taken by the quirk of destiny. The negatively charged people under this number cause a lot of bloodshed and they are at loggerheads with law, only to meet a gruesome death later in their lives. The stubbornness that characterizes the number 26 becomes the cause of all the disasters they face, when they fall prey to the "negative" vibrations of this fateful number! This is one number in Numerology which baffles everybody, because of its manifestation of myriad characters born under it, one different from the other in effect!

People born under Birth Number 8 (8th, 17th and 26th of any month) and with various Destiny Numbers will find their lives as follows:

BIRTH NUMBER 8 & DESTINY NUMBER 1 (SATURN -SUN)

This combination of perseverance and authority helps the natives to become important people in whichever sphere of life they are placed. They work hard and achieve success. When they achieve success, life becomes insipid and either they hardly enjoy the fruits of their labour or someone else enjoys the benefit of their labour. Numero-occultism does not view the combination of 8 and 1 as favourable, more especially in the fields of politics and military where fast computation of strategies and tact are required in addition to hard work and exercise of authority. That pre-requisite to success makes the 8&1 people's lives rather difficult! Their action is delayed and so success also is denied. But who cares...! They do not repent for having "missed the bus". Positive or negative, whatsoever may be their quality, they are plain in their thought and action and are philosophic about the result of their action. They strongly believe in KARMA and get themselves carried away by the current of destiny which actually **makes them victims of others' machinations and manipulations.**

MY FORTUNE

There are some peculiarities found in their outlook and behaviour. They forget that there is more than one option to choose before they act. Their basically biased minds do not accept that there is one more side to the globe, -the darker side. They plunge headlong into whatever pursuit they have in mind which, if positive and harmonious to their numbers, gives astounding success. If negative, it spells their doom!

If the 8 and 1 combination can be rid of the ultra-conservatism or headstrong attitude, the people who are signified by it are admired, adored and in extreme cases, even worshipped. But, mind you, it is not so in the case of politics or military. In the fields of literature, media, religion and philosophy (of any nature), they excel very well and become popular. There is one thing in common between the positive and negative types - they slip at one stage or the other in their lives due to their extreme ideological attachment or due to unforeseen impediment in their career. Those who recover are really lucky ones whose Name Numbers are bound to be lucky!

★ Newsmakers of 8 & 1:

H.F.Verwoerd
(Pro-Apartheid South African P.M.)

Nicolae Ceausescu
(Dictator of Romania killed in 1989)

Francis Gary Powers
(American U-2 Pilot caught by Russians)

Henry Baker
(English naturalist)

Lou Tellegen
(Dutch silent film and stage actor)

Charles Reade
(English Novelist)

NUMBER 8 - SATURN
BIRTH NUMBER 8 & DESTINY NUMBER 2 (SATURN - MOON)

Saturn's vibrations combined with those of Moon do not favour all the natives of this category. Since Moon is a satellite of the earth and it receives it radiance from the Sun, the results of such a combination are somewhat similar to those of Saturn-Sun team. But there are some marked differences too. Number 8's slow pace is sometimes more accentuated or converted into a faster one depending upon the waxing and waning of Moon, thus causing a situation of uncertainty in the prospects of the 8 & 2 people. It is a matter of interest that a vast majority of the people under this combination follow the destinies of their corollary, i.e., 2 & 8 combination, though there is no rule of thumb to such effect in other cases.

The axiom, "one can reach any height, but cannot live there for long!" - is very much applicable to certain categories of Number 8, especially to Number 8 & 2 combination. Generally, some peculiar events in their married or love life are bound to happen. In politics or statecraft their lives will be similar to "rope-walking". If they are military leaders, they should be more careful in planning the strategies, because the slow and contemplative Saturn combined with the unsteady, fickle-minded Moon may impede "action" while it is most necessary and urgent. Those born under this combination pursuing trade or commerce are shining well when they have agro- products, seasonal produce, minerals and occult sciences as their commodities or services to sell. Some of these people choose an off-beat career and shine well! However, in many cases politics or diplomatic career does not seem to be their cup of tea, because they do "costly" mistakes! In the fields of literature, Yoga, philosophy and travels or sports they prove their worth and attain fame. Indecisiveness or hasty decisions must be avoided or else they face unforeseen dangers from which they may not escape. If Name Numbers are good there is no pitfall in any walk of life.

Noteworthy are the lives of the undermentioned Number 8 & 2 people:

★ Newsmakers of 8 & 2:

Michael Jordan (Professional Basketball Player)

Jules Verne (French author famous for his science fiction)

Mohammad Reza Shah Pahlavi
(Iranian Shah overthrown by Ayatollah Khomeini)

Sirimavo Bandaranaike
(The world's first ever woman P.M. of a country
-Srilankan Politician)

Geet Sethi
(Indian Billiards Champion of World fame)

Sally Ride
(First American Woman to orbit the earth)

BIRTH NUMBER 8 & DESTINY NUMBER 3
(SATURN - JUPITER)

Hard work plus hard work, endurance plus endurance, discipline plus discipline ..... you can go on describing this combination of Numbers 8 and 3, except for the fact that the "fatality" of Number 8 (Saturn) overshadows the natives at times. The people under this combination are markedly different from those under the other combinations of Number 8. They work hard and achieve the desired results. Most of them retain the glory of their achievement too unlike others. Their deeds become a permanent feature of history, be it any field they have chosen to venture into. Even those who have not had any remarkable scholastic pursuits or intellectual background, progress in their lives slowly, probably with the sole help of their hidden talents and common sense. Their love of freedom, sense of devotion to the cause they espouse, inventive or innovative ability, loyalty towards friends and interest in the unknown or not-much-known are all the factors which help them become great.

But there is a negative streak in their character too! If the cause or the aim they represent is not an appreciable one, they may not give it up.

It is not because they do not know or foresee the future events. **They just cannot resist the temptation of proving their mettle!** Naturally, there arises a conflict between the mind and the brain. Whether the person is good or bad is decided by the outcome of the conflict. Their habit of "finding fault" with others may be scoffed at, but they are honest and forthright in their opinion. Interestingly, their opinion may be sometimes about their own compatriots or colleagues, but they do not bother! Even when they choose "mild" professions such as poets, writers, singers and the like, only the miseries of human life and decadence of human behaviour attract their attention. In politics, diplomacy or military, they exhibit a strange skill - they exploit the weaknesses of their adversaries rather than enhancing their own strength.

What is surprising is that this policy does help them achieve the desired results. Their philosophy is, "Only a pessimist can be the best optimist!" It is necessary that early grooming of the positive qualities of these people must start. On the other hand, if the negative qualities dominate, the Number 8 & 3 persons cause grievous injuries to the society, although it takes a long time for the world to realise the extent of damage.

★ **Newsmakers of 8 & 3:**

Victor Hugo

Thomas J. Watson Sr.
(Builder of IBM typewriters and data equipment)

Ivan Pavlov (Russian Physiologist)

Swami Chinmayananda
(Journalist - turned – spiritual leader.)

Admiral Sergey Gorshkov (Russian Naval hero)

Mrs.Hillary Clinton
(President Clinton's wife former secretary of state.)

165

BIRTH NUMBER 8 & DESTINY NUMBER 4 [SATURN - URANUS]

Inventions, innovations, impulsiveness, impressive victories, effective communication, and efficient management are the prominent qualities of the people born under 8 & 4 combination of numbers.

The austere, hard-working nature of 8 combined with the outgoing, ever-probing and inventive nature of 4 produces some of the extra-ordinary humans on this earth. There is no subject on this earth which they do not know. They know about every person in their vicinity or neighbourhood and are capable of giving a good account of any place on this planet even though they had not visited it. Their thirst for introducing new or modern techniques, their inventive spirit and their iconoclastic approach, -all prove to be of great interest to those around them. Generally, they are "lone" performers but in any company that suits their taste, they fit in very well. Minds and machines offer wonderful venues to these 8 & 4 people to explore experiment and also excel in.

The personal lives of the people under this combination suffer a jolt in many of the cases. Those who have a harmonious Name Number do not suffer much. But others come across some difficult circumstances which they may not overcome easily. This is common in their love life or married life. Those who are encouraged and supported by some "patrons" find the latter go astray one day for unknown reasons. As for politics or public life where personal friendship and ideology are inseparably entwined, there is a chance that the 8 & 4 people may have to part ways with their companions at one stage. Those who are under negative vibrations face humiliation or even death and those under positive vibrations emerge successful, though their path would not have been so smooth!

Interestingly, the people under this combination with good Name Numbers do not find any obstacle or opposition, especially if they have chosen a "mild" profession connected to poetry, painting or anything related to the human mind. Religion or God is something that calls for extreme action and if anyone is found in that field without an extreme policy, it must be only because of a harmonious Name Number.

Born under the 8 & 4 combination are the following eminent persons who share many common traits:

★ **Newsmakers of 8 & 4:**

Richard I ("The Lion heart"; King of England and crusader)

Danton (French revolution hero)

Antoine Lavoisier (French Chemist)

Emile Coue (Psychotherapist)

Charles Richter (Seismologist)

Robert Frost (American Poet)

Akio Morita (Founder of "Sony" Corporation)

W. Messerschmitt(German Inventor)

BIRTH NUMBER 8 & DESTINY NUMBER 5
(SATURN -MERCURY)

The slow-moving Saturn and the fastest of the solar family, Mercury which is very near to Sun, make a paradoxical combination of Numbers 8 and 5 at least outwardly!

Generally, the people under this combination are versatile, secretive and skilled in a variety of professions or art, fast when there is a need but over-confident during vital moments, popular in whichever circles they live in and always enjoying the niceties of life. They are emotional basically but know how to control their feelings. When pent-up feelings burst they become volcanoes, much to the disappointment of the unsuspecting friends and relatives around them. Many of them can cause changes in the society with the help of a gun or a pen! (It is only to conclude that they are capable of handling both the tools skillfully) They have a group of followers in whichever field they are placed. When their Name Numbers play a positive role in their lives, they reach the peak of their profession or field of activity. If the Name Numbers are unfavourable they meet with a tragic end or at least fade away from the scene unceremoniously. This may be due to a streak of the "Saturnine" influence on their lives. Lucky are those who best utilise the positive vibrations of Saturn and find for themselves permanent peace in their lives. Others are the "vacillating" types who do not stick to one ideology or one group of friends or one particular field of action and so undergo a lot of sufferings. This quality may be more accentuated due to wrong or disharmonious Name Numbers or unfavourable dates of commencement of any important ventures.

The amount of hard work these people put in characterise the Saturn's influence in their early days of life and Number 5 helps them enjoy the fruits of their labour.

There is an important feature in their lives. Even those born under this combination but leading an ordinary life, leave a legacy or perform a deed **at one stage or the other** during their lifetime, which becomes a memorial or a monument or at least an example to the posterity. The readers with an aptitude for research into numerological findings would learn that the unfortunate ones under the 8&5 combination could have averted disaster, if they had some idea about the axiom, "Numbers rule the world"!

A galaxy of personalities under Number 8 & 5 combination is given here under:

★ **Newsmakers of 8 & 5 :**

Benjamin Franklin

J.H.Dunant

(Swiss Nobel Laureate who founded the Red Cross)

Swami Sivananda (Founder of "Divine Life Society)

Willis Carrier (Father of Air-conditioning)

Mao Tse-Tung (The Founder-leader of "Red" China)

Eric Stanley Gardner (Detective fiction writer of fame)

BIRTH NUMBER 8 & DESTINY NUMBER 6 (SATURN - VENUS)

This combination of Numbers 8 and 6 is also one of the most interesting numerological wonders. The introvert and secretive Saturn when combined with the romantic and outgoing Venus, brings out rare talents. But, in personal or professional lives these 8 & 6 people become controversial at one stage or the other, much to the embarrassment of their companions or friends and relatives. Whatever they do, they expect them to be result-oriented. There is "art" or a kind of "finesse" even if they kill someone! The "thrill" they cause in the society or in any group of people will remain for a long time. Some of them cause permanent changes, possibly a "volte - face" in their original approach or policy, - yet they succeed! What's more, they hardly care about the criticism that follows. They are born iconoclasts and do not mind or fear taking up any hazardous assignments, come what may!

A numerologist who researches or a student of this science who experiments will wonder why the finer feelings of Venus are not visible in the character of the 8&6 people. But that's it! You will find non-controversial or not so-complicated personalities under 8 & 6 in the fields like cinema, music, religion or philosophy, though the inner struggles or the latent rebellious nature of such a lot may not be known to the outside world.

One important thing about the lives of Numbers 8 & 6 is that "they do not deceive their own conscience"! When they find another doctrine, place, person or anything that suits their liking but quite opposite to what they had so far cherished in their hearts, **they do not hesitate to choose it!** No doubt, their lives are riddled with ups and downs, which also, could be exploited to their advantage, if the Name Numbers favour it. Any disharmony between the Birth and Destiny Numbers or Name Numbers may upset the numerological equilibrium and danger to the native could be foreseen.

The Saturn -Venus combination of Numbers 8 & 6 consists of interesting personalities:

★ **Newsmakers of 8 & 6 :**

T.S.Eliot (A rebellious writer in English; Nobel Laureate)

Alfred Krupp ("Cannon King"-German Firearms manufacturer)

J.R.Jayawardene (Barrister; President of Srilanka)

W.G.Wilson (Founder of "Alcoholics Anonymous")

Dr.Christiaan Barnard

(South African Surgeon who did the first heart transplant)

M.F.Husain (Painter; film producer)

Robert De Niro (Hollywood actor)

BIRTH NUMBER 8 & DESTINY NUMBER 7
[SATURN - NEPTUNE]

The intuitive and philosophic but sometimes dogmatic Number 7 while under the combination with Number 8 as the Birth Number causes the emergence of personalities who are either worshipped or feared. But the common quality that binds the planets Saturn and Neptune is the high regard with which others endorse the presence of those natives.

The persons born under Number 8 & 7 combination are basically secretive but achieve a lot when they avoid solitude and mix up with others around. They have a strong love of justice but when they themselves go astray from their principle, the world comes to know how bad a person could be! They pray, write, preach, invent and fight, but all the same, they have a unique style of functioning and it is difficult for others to judge what comes next!

The pity is that they themselves would be unable to judge their own future though the destiny's cards lay open on the table. They start very well as one among the team but get disenchanted soon for want of freedom and innovation. They need some new grist to their mills always and so their minds keep on rumbling forever. The turbulence of thoughts spurs them to action. Thus, they become inventors, famous writers or theologians, eminent soldiers or sports persons and efficient administrators. Whatever they do is not going to be devoid of some element of secrecy, uncertainty or some undercurrent of suspense. Many of them have a difficult married life or uncomfortable partnership in their business or profession. On many occasions during their lifetime, they undertake long tours or remain separated from their bases or homes for a long time. Even to their family members or closest associates, they remain a puzzle, though none can underestimate their merits!

The readers will be greatly surprised to know how accurately the aforesaid readings fit into the undermentioned lives of Number 8 & 7 combination:

★ Newsmakers of 8 & 7:

John Wesley (Founder of Methodist Church)

Sir Humphrey Davy (English Cheimist; Inventor)

Larry Ellison

Anthony Blut (British Art critic-turned-spy)

Field Marshal Montgomery (Famous World War II Hero)

Rudolf Hess (German Nazi Leader)

Burton Holmes

Sir James Heath

BIRTH NUMBER 8 & DESTINY NUMBER 8 (SATURN - SATURN)

Astrologically, the planet Saturn is the Lord of two signs of the Zodiac, one being the sign of **Earth** and the other being that of **Air.** In real life too, this 8 & 8 combination offers a lot of opportunities to its natives in any field connected to the said elements. As is always the case with the natives of Saturn, these people also strive hard to carve out a niche for themselves. They struggle with their lives (not necessarily for want of money always!) and achieve some astounding results. Their talents and skills are respected and people look at them with awe and wonder

171

on witnessing their performance. But, the planet Saturn which is ruling both the Birth and Destiny Numbers has a role to play! It causes some kind of "deficiency" in their lives either personal or professional. This cosmological mystery needs a deeper study and thorough research. What is heartening is that these 8 & 8 people take any problems in their stride and forge ahead vigorously.

This is another mysterious side of the Numbers under Saturn's combination. Some of them strike it rich but lose something very valuable. Some others progress very fast in profession but suddenly disappear from the scene of activity. Others have marital problems or health disorders. Unlike the cases under other combinations, this particular one is totally under the "grip of Destiny" and the stories of overcoming it with the help of Freewill are only sporadically heard. The students of Numerology have ample room for research in this combination of 8 & 8 and no doubt, finally would conclude that the Name Numbers of the people under this category **must** be carefully chosen to become lucky.

However, this combination of 8 & 8 should not have any "negative" vibrations, because it would do more harm to the society than the other negative lots. These 8&8 people who can be aptly called "sons of Destiny" are worth remembering for their courage, fortitude and never-say-die attitude.

I hope that the readers do not need more glaring examples under 8 & 8 than those given below!

★ Newsmakers of 8 & 8:

Prince Albert

Sir.A.V.Roe (Founder of AVRO aviation Co.)

Francois Mitterrand (The first Socialist President of France)

William Lear
(One who designed the first commercial jet aircraft)

General MacArthur (American General of W.W. II)

Soichiro Honda (Founder of "Honda" Company)

George Bernard Shaw (English author of rare intellect)

BIRTH NUMBER 8 & DESTINY NUMBER 9 (SATURN - MARS)

There is a peculiar trait with this combination of 8 & 9. The philosopher or the contemplator or the judge under the Birth Number of 8, becomes a "Swashbuckler", "rebel" or a "fighter for a cause" when his Destiny Number is 9! The Martian spirit (or "Martial" spirit) gives the natives a great enterprising quality and a thirst to know more and more. It also helps them to achieve what others consider a dream. Though all the Number 8 people are endowed with the unquenchable spirit of fighting the odds, this quality is augmented by the addition of Number 9. They strive hard, both mentally and physically. In their own lifetime, they see their dreams fulfilled and also find their compatriots enjoying the fruits of their labour. Their style of functioning in any field of activity raises the eyebrows of the observers. In the course of their activity there is a chance that they may get injured by some tools or weapons. In such fields where those things are not used, the Number 8 & 9 people at least suffer humiliation. When these people pass away, the world would think, "why, it is too early to lose a person like him!" But, Destiny's hands are long!

However, it is a matter of interest that these 8 & 9 people leave a legacy to the posterity which is worth remembering.

★ **Newsmakers of 8 & 9:**

John Davison Rockefeller
(American Oil magnate; philanthropist of fame)

Cardinal Messofanti
(R.C.Priest who could speak 58 languages)

Laennec (Inventor of Stethescope)

Carl Gustav Jung (Psychiatrist)

King Bernadotte of Sweden

Mother Teresa
(Albanian nun who got Nobel Prize for her service in India)

Elvis Presley (American Rock Star)

Name numbers and their interpretations

If the value of letters in the name adds up to 8, then the Name number is under the influence of Saturn. Let me list out some general qualities before I give details of each Name number, individually.

If both the birth number and the destiny number are lucky and only if the Name number is 8, its bad impact will ruin the good effects of birth and destiny numbers. They will experience delay in all their ventures. They will never have a contented or mediocre life with comforts. Poverty and disappointments will constantly affect them. Otherwise they could have great wealth, power and authority, meeting with success in whatever they undertake. Even when they are in positions of high rank (outwardly attractive), they will encounter unexpected enmity and frightful responsibilities and can never enjoy the rewards of the positions they occupy. (Saturn enhances their status by making them punish the delinquents. Judges who send scores of people to prison every day belong to this number). Diseases and problems will nag them often. They will never be without some problem or the other. Some avoid marriage, while others get married and suffer. Hence, if somebody, known to you, has this Name number, kindly have it changed immediately.

■ Name No.8: This Name number gives you great success in spiritual life. If they have no control over pleasures, success will be delayed. After a big struggle they may succeed. They will have to face unexpected dangers and difficult circumstances in life.

■ Name No.17: This name number gives demonic qualities while pursuing the goals .It brings many problems and trials. However, they will persistently struggle without giving up. Failures will prompt them to struggle more actively. In the end they will be successful, and they get permanent prosperity and great fame. Some of them risk their lives to attain their goals and so achieve progress. The world can never forget them. This number can give mystic powers also.

NUMBER 8 - SATURN

■ **Name No.26:** This number denotes poverty in old age and fruitless efforts. Those who have this name number undergo great losses due to friends and partners. Circumstances lead them to failure and confusion. This number reduces one's span of life and earns enemies who may even go to the extent of murdering them. Those with Name numbers 26 at first begin their life with great principles and later change their minds and end up only in pursuit of money and status. (Based on their general qualities of number 8, they will be a little more fortunate in their later years).

■ **Name No.35:** This number outwardly seems to be fortunate but the person will suffer losses because of friends and associates. These people will become very rich and popular but later lose all their money. Unexpected accidents may happen. This number helps in earning money through illegal means. Today's friends will become tomorrow's foes. They are very fickle - minded. Expenses will mount. This number would create severe incurable pain in the stomach. (For those with heart problems, this Name number will be a curative factor). Those with this name number must be very careful in their large business endeavours.

■ **Name No.44:** This number helps in earning money easily. Industries involving many people, like cinema theatres, printing presses, coal and iron mining, painting, making of furniture and sports goods, and organizing contests will help them earn a good income. Hiring out vehicles like buses, trucks and cars will also be rewarding. They can also run banks. One day everything may come to a halt. Only the owner will enjoy the profits in a proprietary concern. There is danger from fire and collapse of building. This number indicates that they may have to spend some time in prison. Their minds will go astray towards bad ways. Their lives may be comfortable outside prison. Generally, either they suffer from some disease or spend some time in prison, especially when the birth and destiny numbers are also not harmonious.

175

■ **Name No.53**: They experience success and failure in the beginning of life itself. As they grow older, their lives will become steadier and they will become well-known. Though they are intelligent, they are bound to get into problems beyond their control. These people, who can convert failure into success, will perform good deeds and earn prestige and popularity. (This is an unstable number. Only if the birth number is favourable, will it bring desirable effects). They will be lucky in their old age.

■ **Name No.62**: Generally it will give great fame, victories and a comfortable life. At times, great dangers and failures alternatively affect them. It could bring about serious enmity. It also causes misunderstanding among relatives. Family life will not be pleasant. Intellectual faculties will improve. These people can charm everyone easily. This name number helps in charming enemies too!

■ **Name No.71**: This number which brings about obstacles initially will later shower prosperity. They will be good counselors to others because of their intelligence. This number may be considered fortunate.

■ **Name No.80**: This number has strange mystic powers, but may lead to grave dangers if the date of birth is not favourable. Research in theology will be successful. Nature will change its course and help them. Though their lives are full of dangers and anxieties, they will be comfortable. Miracles will happen. It is a fortunate number.

■ **Name No.89**: This number, which also signifies benefits, brings problems initially. They have a helping tendency and they will acquire great riches like land, houses and jewellery. Women are attracted to them easily. Society will respect the women of this Name number. They have a combination of beauty and wealth. They lead fearless lives with the help of their great power of speech and action. Initially, fire accidents may occur in their lives.

■ **Name No.98:** Like the people under Number 71, these people are also intelligent. But their lives are filled with worries and desires. Though they are intelligent, they may not benefit from that quality. Difficulties and chronic diseases may affect them.

■ **Name No.107:** This number will bring fame and success. If they are men, they will have problems due to women and if they are women, it will be from men. Even if they attain wealth, life will not be comfortable. However, they will be famous and influential.

LOVE AND MARRIAGE

FOR THOSE BORN ON THE 8th, 17th AND 26th OF ANY MONTH

Saturn is your planet. One of the beautiful planets in the galaxy, called the "ringed wonder", it is also considered a natural malefic in the world of predictive sciences. Very few know that Saturn could be a "functional benefic" in people's lives, especially when it relates to love or marriage. Those who are not married at all, those who have serious marital problems and those who do not find suitable life partners mostly fall into this category. We would only advise them to have lucky name numbers and correct the course of their fate! The science of Numerology has many success stories under Number 8 and you only need to consult this book or the practitioner!

Your number is 8. You have a natural attraction towards those born on the 8th and its series. In general, number 1, 4 and 8 persons attract you and if you are married to one of them, you will be happy.

Passively reacting to the vibrations of number 8 people are numbers 3, 5 and 6. With a policy of "give & take" and favourable numbers, even these numbers are fit for peaceful and lasting relationship.

It is advised that persons born on the dates of 2nd, 7th, 9th and their series be avoided for long term emotional relationships or marriage. As such, the suggestions to Number 8 persons regarding their relationships are to be carefully studied and given. Numbers 2, 7 and 9 may add to the problems of Number 8 people. So caution is necessary!

MY FORTUNE

MISCELLANY

Those born on dates 8, 17 and 26 need not fear the vagaries of Destiny. They can choose a lucky date with a lucky number and continue doing all auspicious things on such dates. Dates 1, 10, 19 and 28 (28th should be reservedly used) are lucky dates for them; the dates with a combined total of the numbers in any date (Destiny Number) amounting to 1 are also lucky. 4, 13, 22, 31 will confer favourable results. (But 4 causes unexpected changes also) 9, 18 and 27 are also good provided their impact must be fully utilised.

Avoid 8, 17 and 26. Any combination of 8 is not good at all.

The 8 people are advised to use Yellow color in their dresses. Dark green and blue are reportedly favourable, Do avoid Black, brown and red.

Blue stones (Sapphire and the like) with 6 sutras (cemophanic lines) are the best suitable lucky stones for them. They must wear it in open setting. They must choose faultless stones because their destiny is always vulnerable to changes.

In business, those born on the date totalling to 1 or 4 will be helpful; 8 people also assist well, provided their Destiny or Name Numbers are not harmful.

NUMBERS AND NEWS

Number 8 has a special significance both in Hinduism and Islam. "Ashta Aishwarya" -the eight types of wealth for a happy life is the ultimate in material success as said in Hinduism. Islam says that there are eight paradises awaiting a devout and righteous person in the celestial heaven. The basic and the most powerful element -LIGHT, takes 8 minutes from the Sun to reach the Earth and the practitioners of Tantra or Magic in India, invariably follow 8 procedures (Ashta Karma)!

NUMBER 9 - MARS

The red and fiery planet nearest to the earth and the fourth from sun in the celestial orbit is MARS. There are many stories afloat about the arrival of Martians on our planet, but now we know that the Americans have successfully landed their craft recently on the Martian surface and we are able to view its terrain through our TV sets. Thus the folklore and the myths about Mars have suffered a jolt! What is surprising is that the astronomers and astrologers as well, who belonged to the yester years, be it from ancient India, Egypt or Greece, were able to give a convincing report about the Martian surface's colour, the planet's speed, various events connected to its transit in the sky and the like,-even without a known or chronicled scientific instrument! Numerology has assigned Number 9 to Mars symbolically and let us discuss its role in human lives.

The Number 9 people - Martians as we may call them, who were born on the 9th, 18th and 27th of any month are courageous, aggressive, dashing and fearless. They make good soldiers, lawyers, adventurers, engineers, sports persons, and even crowd -pulling politicians! Number 9 causes restlessness and so these people are always busy,-both physically and mentally. They are revolutionaries in their own style in any walk of life they choose, even if it is going to be the profession of a poet, a spiritual leader, or that of a film maker. They are good organisers and disciplined administrators who do not shirk their duties and responsibilities. Power in any form is their aim and hard work is their way of life. Generally, they have robust health and are with a good circulation of blood in their physique. They love animals (so long as they serve their purpose) and also vehicles. Though outwardly they seem to be tough, obstinate and crude, they are very romantic and could be more sympathetic than even the people of other Numbers. They only need to be convinced of what they should do. They have an inventive and innovative ability which helps them become great scientists or surgeons (who use implements like knife, screw drivers etc. made of iron or steel and also chemicals). Many of them fit in very well as soldiers and achieve glory and Number 9, either as their Birth Number or Destiny Number, are bound to display such qualities. The society would look at them with awe and respect.

Those with the negative vibrations of Number 9 are the Martians of dangerous pursuits and they cause a lot of suffering to others and also to themselves. They are cruel, haste, quarrelsome and of rebellious nature. They are passionate and involve themselves in illicit love affairs. They always have a problem with the opposite sex and hardly listen to anyone's advice. Injuries by weapon, (or getting a permanent scar on their bodies due to surgery) chemicals or explosives is something that happens in their lives at one point of time or the other. Their impulsive nature not only lands them in predicaments in which they suffer a loss or a jail term or an accident causing a grievous injury. This negatively oriented 9-people also become a danger to the society and they would resort to any despicable means to serve their own ends. Even those who develop such morbid tendencies surprisingly turn over a new leaf in their lives, when their Destiny Number is good and harmonious. On following the correct numerological advice to choose the right numbers for their names and by following sincerely such an advice, phenomenal changes have occurred in their lives and the so-called "bad people" have even become "saints" in their outlook and behaviour.

Positive or Negative, both should avoid over-spending, over-eating and overreacting, to lead a healthy and wealthy life. Moderation will balance their emotions. But in any noble efforts they need not lack courage and vigorous action!

NUMBER 9 - MARS

The number 9 people or the martial "Martians" are emotional rope walkers! They must ensure that their mental vibrations and bio-rhythms could either aid their actions positively if they are noble-hearted or act against their evil intentions. Unlike some combinations, the 9 people do not possess a "fatalistic" feeling. Good or bad, they choose their path knowingly and are ready to face the result of their actions. So, the struggles of their everyday life make them more tenacious which makes the world think that they are great. **Interestingly, when at least two people under Number 9 follow the same path in any field of activity, you will find them each using his or her own ways and means to achieve the goal!** This peculiar and original trait of Number 9 proves that they are the people who leave an indelible saga in the history of mankind.

The great planetary physicists, Dr.Fred Hoyle of Cambridge and Dr.Shklovsky of Russia who had researched a lot into the mysterious forces of Mars and its "moons" in the 1960s, had expressed their surprise as to how the ancient astrologers had precisely known the influences of this "Red planet" long before. (Ref. "How the stars influence your mind and health" published in the journal "Science & Mechanics" in 1968). Number 9 folks! Remember! Your Planet is MARS!

What the Birth Dates signify

■ Date - 9   On this Martian date of birth are born a wide variety of persons, the walk of life of each differing from the other, but good or bad, they are all fiercely independent and enterprising. Unlike those of other ruling planets, these people display an innate desire to do something revolutionary. They are born "doers" and once they decide to do something they never change their plans, come what may! They meticulously plan and carefully execute their work. The typically Martian trait in them forces them to act bravely in the face of danger or opposition to their plans, though sometimes their actions are considered foolhardy. Kings, heads of state and military leaders who are in commanding position, generally do not change their original plans and find it too late to do it, thus becoming victims of their own plans. Businessmen, scientists, inventors, writers and those in the field of fine arts have a lot of time to rethink on their strategy and so they escape disaster. A few of this latter group leave immortal legacies before they depart, but a few of the former group sometimes lose their lives even. Interestingly, political leaders born on this date seem to have always some contingency plans and come out clean!

■ Date – 18   There are two types of people usually found to be born on this date. The first types are ruled by their minds and fall into deep chasms of trouble with their eyes open, sometimes even losing their lives or honour in the bargain. They might belong to royal families, politics or religion. The second types are those ruled by their brains and they watch their steps and tread cautiously. They generally belong to the fields of science, literature, sports or the tinsel world of cinema and are more organized and ready to change their policy or strategy. Those who are established in business, interestingly enough, may be phenomenally successful, provided their destiny and name numbers are lucky. Although people born on any date are bound to face serious problems when they fail to control their senses, it affects the most of those born on the 18th. When they are morally upright, they are worshipped. If they go wayward, they pay a heavy price to buy peace of mind and honour. However, nobody is an exception to the vagaries of destiny and if the name numbers are weak and unharmonious, they face humiliation and suffering. Those born on the 18th of any month of the year are found to be successful in their careers or love life. They are the people who used both their brains and brawns in the right direction!

■ Date – 27   Though this birth date denotes strength and success, there are variations caused by destiny and name numbers. If they are mutually harmonious, the efforts of those born on the 27th will bear fruit. No field of activity is an exception to them. In religion, politics and business, they achieve great success. People who take extreme action would come to suffer soon, though some of them are immortalized in the annals of history. The number 27 in the birth date signifies by itself the combination of Moon and Neptune and so success in entertainment industry. It also gives intuitive power and the world would wonder one day how these people fought the odds and succeeded in their lives. Those who look soft and meek should not be mistaken for innocent and weak people. They could be biding their time to explode, nobody knows when! When it comes to the question of money, they work hard and not only earn but also invest in profitable business. Those who are born on the 27th and take to religion at a very young age, realize their calling and excel many others in their service to god and the humans as well.

People born under Birth Number 9 (9th, 18th and 27th of any month) and with various Destiny Numbers will find their lives as follows:

BIRTH NUMBER 9 & DESTINY NUMBER 1 (MARS -SUN)

Placed between the Earth and the Jupiter, the most speculated planet in the field of science, Mars is represented by Number 9 the qualities of which have been already discussed. When Number 9 is in numerological conjunction with Number 1, that is SUN, they both are mutually helpful. Number 9 executes meticulously all the plans and ideas of the Number 1. The energetic and enthusiastic No. 9 people get a boost in their leadership qualities when combined with Number 1. They become inventive and also innovative. This quality consolidates their status in their professional lives and thus they earn the respect of others. Since 9 and 1 are naturally harmonious to each other, money and comforts in life flow easily their way. However, in the early part of the life, strife and struggles cannot be ruled out. Their family ties are strong and in making their livelihood, the family ties or connections play an important role usually (of course, even in undoing also!). There is always a majestic behaviour that is externally visible to the outside world, though the latter may not know the bottled up emotions beneath or the pent-up feelings. Unlike the combinations of other Numbers, 9 & 1 will find one day that the self-control they possessed suddenly gets evaporated and one can very well guess the result! However, 9 & 1 can exude more warmth not only in their words but also in their actions. When many others under different numbers could only do lip-service, 9 & 1 people serve the society with their heart and soul.

When we discuss about the negative lot under Number 9 & 1 category, there is only one point to talk about. **Do Listen to good advice and act accordingly!.** The cause of your ruin may be your personal relations with people, especially with the opposite sex. When you choose your life partner see that he or she is not hot-tempered or arrogant, because such qualities worsen the situation. So must you judge your business partners and your staff or servants. Many good lives have been marred by wrong and disharmonious numbers getting connected to the combination of Numbers 9 and 1.

★ **Newsmakers of 9 & 1:**

Volta (Scientist)

Karel Capek (Czech Novelist)

Cardinal Richelieu (French Clergy & Statesman)

J.A. Wheeler (Physicist who developed Hydrogen bomb)

Ralph Nader (Consumers advocate)

Katie Holmes

Zakir Hussain (Tabla maestro)

BIRTH NUMBER 9 & DESTINY NUMBER 2 (MARS - MOON)

The aggressive Number 9 (Mars) and the over-sensitive Number 2 (Moon) are numerologically not quite good for partnership, though the astrological relations are friendly. However, when Destiny unites a Number 2 man and a Number 9 girl in wedlock or when Number 9 people choose Number 2 people for business partnership, there comes an unexpected disharmony. When their Name numbers are also negative to each other, hell may break loose! Hence any remedy that is necessary is to be done can be done only with the help of Name Numbers!

Just as the numbers of the combination are, the lives of 9 & 2 people are also a mixture of the opposites. Controversies in their behaviour, profession, their service or help to others, or their relations with others (especially opposite sex), always crop up and nag them. It is a paradox rather against the maxim, "Unlike poles attract each other"! The controversies play a more important role in the lives of those with the negative vibrations and the 9 & 2 people with the positive influence do not suffer much. However, the "Martians" who are not quite adaptable and are dominative types find themselves happy on Number 2 days or with Number 2 people or in business connected to Number 2, provided they are "positively" swung and have lucky Name Numbers. This peculiarity must be observed before anyone judges the 9 & 2 lot.

In politics, the 9 & 2 people either suffer themselves or make others suffer. The streak of selfishness in them surfaces and they stand exposed. But the legacy they leave for the posterity is a long-lasting one! This point is applicable to the field of religion also, of course, in a positive manner. In military, they become good strategists and more tenacious. They fear none even if it comes to over-looking the orders of their superiors. Their main aim is to safeguard a common interest. They make supreme sacrifices if need be. There may be 9 & 2 people in various fields but even when there is no necessity to resist, fight or assert themselves strongly in "milder" issues (where tact could easily solve the problem), they still take up the cudgel! If this habit is held under control, they become great saints, diplomats, caring husbands and successful lawyers or politicians.

★ Newsmakers of 9 & 2 :

Mozart (Austrian Composer)

W.H. Harrison
(9th U.S. President, died on th 36th day of his Presidency)

Henry Kissinger (U.S. Statesman)

Samuel Chung Ting (U.S. Scientist; Nobel Laureate)
Patrick.C. Steptoe
(British Scientist who produced the first test tube baby)

Yuri Gagarin (The first man in space)

Bobby Fischer

BIRTH NUMBER 9 & DESTINY NUMBER 3 (MARS - JUPITER)

The Numbers 9 and 3, when they come as the Birth and Destiny Numbers respectively constitute one of the lucky combinations in Numerology, subject to the strength of Name Numbers. This combination provides extraordinary administrative capacity to be a leader of unusual strength to work hard and achieve more. Even the little trace of selfishness or euphemistically calling, "practical" attitude of Number 9 is sidelined by the effect of Number 3. The grim and business-like approach of Number 9 is softened by the ever-youthful and smiling Jupiterian Number 3. Both the numbers help the native to grow and develop any business and help the mankind and also themselves through the same. "Live and let live" will be their policy. However hectic their routine activities may be, they have time to think of the down-trodden or an entertainment or some social service.

Though most of these people are found in manufacturing businesses, you must know that they are basically inventors or innovators "who keep the world going" in the literal sense. That is to say that in designing vehicles - be they for use on ground or in the air, they make a mark for themselves. Even in uniformed services where hard work and discipline are very important, any activities connected to music or theatre also attract them. In politics or statecraft, they become victims of the machinations of their own compatriots.They either quit the post on a scandal or else quit the world altogether, though the effect differs from case to case. (That's where the Name Numbers would play an important role to mitigate the negative effect). There is a "knack" with them that helps them to become "important" people in the world, although they may not themselves know that they possess it! Money, opportunities, comfort, - all flow in when everything is set to order, but they may all go away when they do not heed good advice or when they act in haste.

Have a look at this important and lucky combinations by going through the list of people born under it:

★ **Newsmakers of 9 & 3:**

Sir George Cayley (English Designer of the first glider)

Gail Borden
(American businessman-philanthropist who invented how to condense milk)

V.M. Molotov
(Russian diplomat and inventor of "Molotov Cocktails" during World War II)

David Sarnoff
(American broadcaster who continuously for 72 hrs. transmitted "Titanic'"'s distress signal)

Wilhelm Maybach (German designer of Mercedez Benz)

W.C. Rontgen
(He won the first Nobel prize for Physics; Discovered X-rays)

Sir F.H. Royce
(English manufacturer of Rolls-Royce cars and aero-engines)

BIRTH NUMBER 9 & DESTINY NUMBER 4 [MARS - URANUS]

This is a combination of two planets unfriendly to each other. I am unable to call them "inimically disposed", because in my experience, I have found out that on a couple of fronts, those under this 9 & 4 combinations have achieved what those under different other combinations could not do. Readers by now would have understood that even naturally benefic numbers (planets) when they become Birth and Destiny Numbers of a person (or vice versa) **need not always confer** favourable results..

The combination of 9 & 4 are capable of doing or undoing anything. The critical, analytical and suspicious Destiny Number 4 influences the courageous go-getter born on any 9-days and thus the latter finds it hard to proceed in any issue without hesitation. But, positively speaking, the aggressiveness and the executive ability of the "Martians" which are imperative in any issue concerning a group, society or a country get a boost due to the positive influence of Number 4. Generally, they do things which stir up emotions and controversies, but they have no axe to grind and their interest is only to safeguard something which is of paramount importance.

187

They do not cheat their conscience because they are capable of changing their strategies if need be! They don't care for public opinion because they always have their own loyal followers. In politics and military, they either cause a drastic change or they themselves become cause of a change! There are many successful people born under this combination in the field of histrionics or music.

Strangely enough, the negative types under this combination of numbers do not expose themselves much. They are secretive and have limited but trusted company. If they are inventors, they spend more time in designing WMD (weapons of mass Destruction!). They bear grudges and do not forgive or forget if they are wronged. Sex plays an important role in their emotional or personal life (some choose it in one form or the other as they chose their "Profession" too).

The undermentioned personalities of the world who are in our Numerological net are those born under Numbers 9&4:

★ **Newsmakers of 9 & 4:**

Peter the Great (Tsar of Russia)

Samuel Finley Breese Morse (Inventor)

Ernst Mach (Austrian Physicist)

Stephen.G.Cleveland (22nd U.S. President)

James S.McDonnell (Aircraft manufacturer)

Hugh Hefner (Publisher of "Play boy")

BIRTH NUMBER 9 & DESTINY NUMBER 5 (MARS - MERCURY)

Mercury, represented by Number 5 is not a friendly planet as far as Mars (Number 9) is concerned. But Number 9 is not inimical or of anti-vibrations as far as Number 5 is concerned. When a person's Birth and Destiny Numbers are 9 and 5 respectively, controversies are bound to rise. They still carve a niche for themselves despite odds they face in their lives which mystery can be analysed by thorough research. May be, by a coincidence or due to their intuitive ability which comes through a favourable Number 5, they naturally avoid the Number 2 dates and do not choose for marriage those born on the 1st, 2nd, or the 8th of any month. The unsuccessful under this combination would find that their Name Numbers are also unfavourable!

As with any No. 9-person, 9 & 5 -person also takes an optimistic view when confronted with problems. His Destiny Number gives him speed, ability to plan strategies, hardworking nature and a high degree of adaptability. But this lot tend to take unusual risks which lands them in unforeseen problems. One may think why the intuition failed these people. They have an innate skill in managing any crisis but **sometimes** they overestimate their capabilities. The brash nature that arises out of the Birth Number 9 is somewhat balanced by Number 5 and many people under this combination have succeeded in politics, a field which demands extra-ordinary diplomacy, if not cunning! Generally, you would find those successful ones having acted in too risky a way to speak openly about. Others make use of the best qualities of Mercury and make their own lives successful. Those who brave a society or a political party bide their time and attack at the ripe moment. They are autocratic sometimes but they alone know which card they must play to succeed in life. There is always an element of rebellious nature in their activities, but it is only that quality which distinguishes them from others. They are remembered by their countries in some cases, even for their "negative" attitude or deal. Physical or mental sufferings are taken in their stride and so their names become legends in the history. Even in a field of activity or vocation where they need not use force, weapons or violence, they prove to be "off-beat" in their function or "out-of-the-earth"!

Those who do not have favourable Name Numbers or those who choose dates of disharmonious numbers, find their lives miserable. Humiliation, loss of money or even loss of limbs or life are common among those people. Unlike other combinations, this particular one -if not harmoniously set, causes a permanent damage which is irreparable. The numerological history can cite umpteen examples of those who were **"forearmed because they were forewarned!"**

★ Newsmakers of 9 & 5:

Amerigo Vespucci (Discoverer of America)

George Stephenson (Inventor of Steam engine)

Helen Keller
(Deaf, dumb and blind woman who could still communicate)

Theodore Roosevelt (U.S. President; 1906 Nobel Laureate)
John Brown (American anti-slavery crusader)

Bertrand Russel

BIRTH NUMBER 9 & DESTINY NUMBER 6 (MARS -VENUS)

Number 9 (Mars) people with Number 6 (Venus) as their Destiny Number do rather well in fields such as, literature, cinema and research-oriented studies. Politics does not offer always a successful career. It may be due to the fact that 9 and 6, though astrologically neutral, do not confer better results, since 6 opposes the vibrations of 9 when it comes to **politics** (which is the domain of Sun which demands "real" hard work for success). The tenacity and active disposition of 9 somewhat suffers by the easy-going, comfort-loving 6 thus making the native miss opportunities. But, the positive vibrations of the Number 6 gives the sociability, attractive manners, magnetic personality and the power of glamorous speech to the Number 9 person, which no doubt, are welcome qualities. However, disappointments are not ruled out even when a 9 & 6 person reaches the top in politics.

There is an interesting side to this combination. In the field of histrionics, literary pursuits, any field of philosophy which is purely related to human welfare or the mysteries of the planets it will provide very successful opportunities to them. Mostly they shine amidst competition and rivalry. Sexual exploits leading to scandals or nasty situations may arise. Their sense of independence does not mean that they are unsociable. In their personal lives the 9s are always aided by the 6s, provided they are of **opposite** sexes. They earn a lot but spend it all for vanity and this habit must be kept under control. Though Number 9 people protect others, the influence of 6 gives them a kind of selfish or self-centered attitude. The vigour and youthfulness of the people under this combination will be the talk of the town, even if they are of old age! There is a kind of romantic touch to whatever they do. (No.9 is masculine and No. 6 is feminine and this combination possesses both the qualities). Money flows in easily and if not invested securely, it will disappear at the same speed!

When you visit the numerological world in search of Number 9 & 6 people, you will find the following among them:

★ **Newsmakers of 9 & 6:**

Honore' de Mirabeau (French Politician)

Herbert Spencer (English Sociologist)

Lewis Carroll (Author of "Alice in Wonderland")

Richard Nixon (37th U.S. President; resigned due to scandal)

Chun Doo Hwan (Korean General who later became President)

Marita Koch (Famous German Woman athlete)

BIRTH NUMBER 9 & DESTINY NUMBER 7 [MARS - NEPTUNE]

The combination of numbers 9 and 7 denotes that two inimical forces are united numerologically to make the person a powerful personality. These two planets-Mars and Neptune are enemies to each other, but Neptune gives in to Mars. The practical and forceful Number 9 is ably supported by the mystical and philosophical 7. Hence, the vibrations of both the numbers help the person to fulfill his or her dreams. Even in marriage the Number 9-Man will get a lot of support from Number 7-woman, willingly or unwillingly (It is a paradox but it is also a practical reality!)

MY FORTUNE

The inner meanings of a doctrine, or the function of a system, or the human mind's behaviour, or a machine's operation -are the very subjects taken up by the 9&7 persons for their vocation or pastime. Their style of performance is unique and their minds give priority to "larger" interests of the society or the nation. Their power of concentration in what they do is superb. When those under other combinations of Number 9 are somewhat crude and casual in finishing any task, the 9 & 7 people do it very elegantly. They leave their stamp in whatever they do. Spiritual pursuits sometimes may be impeded by some practical considerations. The welfare of the common man is their paramount concern. Academics, art, administration, philosophy, science or sports -the flexibility of Number 7 gives the fiery and steadfast Number 9 such wide choice of fields to shine in. You would hardly find a wastrel under this combination, because they are active both mentally and physically. If men are 9 and women are 7, their marriage will not pose big problems. Caution must be exercised if it is otherwise. If they choose lucky Name Numbers problems can be kept off. With an unfavourable Name Number and with negative vibrations of Number 7, the Number 9 people will find themselves working hard but not earning anything. Sometimes, such a lot may suddenly fade away from the scene either by death or otherwise.

★ Newsmakers of 9 & 7:

Peter Mark Roget (Author of the first English Thesaurus)

Rudolf Diesel (Inventor of I.C. Engine)

John D. Watson (American Psychologist)

Bruce Lee
("Kung Fu" exponent who became a famous Hollywood Star; Died mysteriously)

Baron de Montesquieu (French Political Philosopher)

King Albert Edward VII

192

NUMBER 9 - MARS
BIRTH NUMBER 9 & DESTINY NUMBER 8 (MARS - SATURN)

The ways of functioning of the planets in the galaxy are quite in order and their mutual relations (influence) are also orderly. When their radiations combinedly influence the earth and the lives on it, myriad forms of human behaviour are brought to light. Thus, the magic of cosmos paves the way for the logic of humans on the earth. That is how we learn the behaviour of the planets also. Under the numerological combination of numbers, Numbers 9 & 8 also present one such strange partnership. Saturn is neutral to Mars, but Mars is an enemy to Saturn. All the same, both are by nature malefic!

The natives are energetic, mentally or physically. They take up responsibilities for the cause of others and get unduly burdened before discharging them. They plan and execute their ideas and doctrines independently, always in their own unique style. The basically less lucky 8 causes some impediments to their progress, but such impediments serve as lessons to the natives in understanding the vagaries of **time** and concentrate their **energy** in their projects with adequate change in strategies. Generally, they are impatient but sooner or later they become adaptable. There will be a lot of ups and downs in their lives which are caused **not** always because of their behaviour or method of function, but because of the undecipherable power of DESTINY. Even in the field of religion or philosophy, they display a quality of militancy. Mostly in their personal lives they are dissatisfied souls. There is always a queer twist to the events in their private life. The losses or setbacks they suffer do not discourage them. They find frequent changes in their careers or strategies but their style of functioning will be one and the same. The positive types are good judges of people and situations and act fast with confidence. The negative ones are suspicious and quarrelsome and are not confident in their approach to problems. As for personal relations, they always have a revolutionary idea and when it comes to the institution of marriage, their views and actions are rather strange. Though money is supposed to come easily to the Number 9s, the partnership with Number 8 gives delay and anxieties. On the other hand, popularity and appreciation for the good work done by them easily come their way!

The negative traits affect the fortune of Number 9 & 8 types very badly. Such people very easily lose friends and support from relatives. They ruin themselves and also become the cause of others' ruin. Some of them become anti-social and can hardly be redeemed from the depths of their sinful life. They may stand a chance if they choose a favourable Name with harmonious numbers; but the earlier, the better!

The list of personalities given here may enlighten the readers about the mysterious forces at work in the lives of 9 & 8 people in a positive manner:

★ Newsmakers of 9 & 8:

Dr.Samuel Johnson (The first lexicographer in English)

Sir.Donald Bradman (The renowned cricketer)

Nelson Mandela
(The black South African civil rights leader who later became President)

Joseph Strauss
(The Engineer who built the Golden Gate Bridge in U.S.A)

Dr.N.E. Shumway
(American Surgeon who did the first heart transplant in U.S.A.)

Ulysses S.Grant (18th President of U.S.A.)

C.Vanderbilt (America's Shipping & Railroad Magnate)

Elizabeth Taylor (Hollywood actress)

BIRTH NUMBER 9 & DESTINY NUMBER 9 (MARS - MARS)

Out of all the combinations which we have discussed earlier, we have **not** seen anyone viewing the life on earth from a totally **practical** standpoint. Number 9 & 9 (Mars & Mars) is the last of the series yet not the least! Unlike others these people either see or experience their lives' images in a practical way. They imagine, visualise or even fantasies but the odds of life always dominate their minds. This queer behaviour may cause anxiety to their relatives, friends or business associates who may even get irritated. That does not affect the mode of thinking or the function of these 9 & 9 people. The planet Mars is at his full strength. Strangely enough, they not only visualise problems but also suggest remedies to them. The paradox about their life, in spite of the scientific or logical bent of their minds, is that in their personal lives, especially when it comes to their marriage, **most** of them do not judge their fate properly, (with correct and harmonious Name Numbers, some of them remedy any fault later and live happily!) However, the lives and works of many of the 9 & 9 types make their entry into the text books of schools and colleges **mostly after their lifetime!** It is because they do not thrust on others what they themselves have not experienced or experimented!

Though they are hard workers and forceful orators or writers, when they are under the total influence of Mars which is both Birth and Destiny numbers, they tend to become foolhardy. They plunge themselves headlong in the service of mankind without minding the damage done to their own selves or institutions. They come to loggerheads with those who may prove to be valuable later. Ironically, their words and deeds build an edifice which remains the cynosure of the public eye and with the same tools they will demolish it also! (They do know that there are "vested interests" that are ready to do that). This habit or trait makes them strange personalities.

Some of them are successful as diplomats and thespians. The reason for their success may be that they must have mastered the art of "acting" which is the mainstay of their profession (I am only citing the words of a retired diplomat and famous orator-writer who is no more!). All others who cannot hide their feelings, who cannot be snobbish and who call a spade a spade, do enjoy the music of life - be it lullaby or elegy! However, all of them are people who face the result of their "Karma" boldly, though their health gets the beating. Caution is necessary, if they retire from active life or become **"do-nothings"** which is **more** harmful!

They must avoid intoxicating drinks or sensitive drugs because their blood takes the shortest time to absorb toxins, since Number 9 (Mars) is directly related to blood. As they spend all their energy and resources for the sake of others whom they care for, they tend to forget their own well-being. These 9 & 9 types are advised to choose any interesting or soul-satisfying hobby or pastime like music, dance, reading looks on yoga or practising it. It may "cool" down their mental and physical dynamos which have been functioning restlessly. As they have a great interest in protecting those placed under them or those who sought their help, they forget to entertain themselves, though basically they are the very "earthly" types who love the finer things of human life.

Since discussing the "negative" types may cause embarrassment, I shall stop at this. Even those "negative" types have a way out. They must remember that Numbers rule the world and they only need to be fine-tuned to find their fortune!

★ **Newsmakers of 9 & 9:**

Joseph Stalin,

John Milton (English Poet)

Galvani (Italian Scientist)

Omar Khayyam (Persian Poet of multi-faceted talents)

Neville Chamberlain (British P.M.)

Yataro Iwasaki (Founder of Mitsubishi)

Edith Cresson (First Woman P.M. of France)

Rudolf Steiner (Austrian philosopher)

Colonel Sanders (KFC)

NAME NUMBERS AND THEIR INTERPRETATIONS

If the value of letters in the name adds up to 9, it will come under the influence of this name number. These people will be more successful than those born on the days of number 9 because this name number helps people born under other numbers to be more energetic, hardworking and intelligent.

NUMBER 9 - MARS

Now let us look at the different name numbers of 9 and their qualities individually.

■ **Name No.9:** If the name comes under this number, it signifies wisdom and capability. It also denotes travel, struggles against odd situations and victory in the end. When they finally succeed, they will have a long life of luxury.

■ **Name No.18:** This name number, which signifies the decline of divinity, will bring in problems, procrastination in all matters, deviousness, and dangerous enemies. Their selfishness may include them to indulge in antisocial activities. They follow evil ways consciously and become highly selfish. Life devoid of peace and rest will be the order of the day. This number signifies growth of personal desires at the cost of virtue. Desires will come to an end. Divine grace will get destroyed. This number, which denotes jealousy, malice and dangers due to fire and weapons, is not considered desirable.

■ **Name No.27:** This number signifies a clear mind and intelligence, unceasing hard work, accumulation of wealth, all round influence and positions of prominence and high rank. Especially in uniformed services like police, army, etc., they will rise very high in their ranks. This is as fortunate as number 24, which has been explained earlier in this book. They will be respected and treated as the best in their profession or service. They like to do social service and will be involved also in matters that would benefit them. This is a very fortunate number that brings spirituality and magical powers.

■ **Name No.36:** This number can raise even poor people to an enviable status and make them live in mansions. Only when these people go away from their place of birth to distant regions, do they attain success. They will travel extensively and occupy high positions. This number, though it appears very fortunate, will cause problems within the family. They may be surrounded by disloyal people.

197

■ **Name No.45:** This is a lucky Name number. Even those who struggle at lower levels will rise to a higher status and positions. They are good conversationalists and will be found in gatherings that involve entertaining people. These hard-working people will earn outstanding positions in their career. They will achieve their goals at any cost. People would wonder if their life was a big show. Even though they may have nagging problems, they will retain their smile and will never allow anyone to know their problems. This number, which assures a comfortable life, fame and wealth, is a desirable one. Diseases will also be cured.

■ **Name No.54:** This number will give success step by step. Failures may also happen. They may begin their lives with prestige, reputation and prosperity. Stubbornness and thoughtless decisions will make them lose their name and fame. Greed is their worst enemy that could make them lose all their wealth if they are not careful. In the fag end of their lives, they may achieve peace and success. Their life will be without freedom and they will be under the control of others.

■ **Name No.63:** This is also a lucky number. However, if this comes as a Name number, it might lead one to wrong path. The ancient texts describe this number as one related to devious means, so the less said, the better!

■ **Name No.72:** This is the best of all numbers under 9. Although these people struggle in their early years, they later enjoy life with all comforts. A mind devoid of doubt will be filled with joy. The wealth acquired by these people will remain intact in their family for many future generations. Money keeps on coming continuously, without fail. (Businessmen should take note of this advantageous number). It will also bring repute. This number signifies permanent wealth.

■ **Name No. 81:** This number signifies a fortunate life. This will give development, good position and wealth. If these people are not careful, their luck could change for the worse. They will have opportunities to become teachers.

NUMBER 9 - MARS

■ **Name No.90:** As this number derives its full power from number 9, its people will go to any extent to get their desires fulfilled. Victory will be certain. They will become very wealthy and famous. For those who are interested in spiritual pursuits this number is not desirable.

■ **Name No.99:** This Name number will lure its native to devious ways. Success will come along with enmity. This number signifies being attacked by enemies, and hence it is not a good number. (However they will be blessed with education, wealth and prosperity).

■ **Name No.108:** This number can give high positions and success. Everything will happen according to their desire. As this number induces its people to make good efforts resulting in success, it is a very lucky number.

LOVE AND MARRIAGE

FOR THOSE BORN ON THE 9th, 18th AND 27th OF ANY MONTH

Mars is your planet. If there is one planet in our galaxy which has kindled the imagination of scientists, fiction writers and astrologers as well, it is nothing but Mars! In astrology, it is feared as a malefic planet which is believed to cause hurdles to a happy married life. The "positive" ones born on the "Martian" dates display vigour and energy and work harder than people of other numbers. The "negative" ones are quarrelsome and foolhardy. When it comes to emotional relationships or marriage, these Number 9 persons take a lot of risk and gamble with their lives. Some succeed and some others don't! But Martians keep going unmindful of the result!

You, the Number 9 people have a natural attraction (which is also mutual) with those born on the 3rd, 5th, 6th and 9th and their series of dates. Their vibrations work well to lead a harmonious love life or married life. These Number 9 persons would find their relations with those born on the 4th, 7th and their series of dates as neutral or passive. They could fraternize or live together with some degree of adaptability.

199

It is better for these "Martians" to avoid those born on the 1st, 2nd and 8th and their series of dates for a long term relation like marriage. If you go in for such a relation wittingly or unwittingly, problems arise soon and upset the harmony and peace.

MISCELLANY

All those who were born on the dates of Number 9 (9th, 18lh and 27th of any month) will find the 5th, 14th, 23rd, 9th, 18th, 6th, 15th, 21st, 24th, 27th and 30th of any month lucky. If they carry out important work on those days, they are sure to succeed and will achieve their noble goals. 1st, 10th and 27th will also be favourable. It is better that they do not choose the 2nd, 11th, 20th and 29th which are unlucky for persons born on the dates of 9.

The lucky colour for the Number 9 is red, crimson or reddish purple. It gives a strong will-power and an active mind and body. They should avoid Pale green and white and such light colours that are not quite lucky.

The 9s will naturally find the gemstone Coral or Bloodstone to be helpful in keeping off diseases connected to their blood, skin and also the debilitating Parkinson's disease. They are to wear the stone next to their skin in any manner.

The persons born on 9-dates would choose professions related to civil engineering (construction), manufacture and sale of steel goods or machinery. Armed forces or Diplomatic missions or law will be other venues of their operation. Number 9 (Mars) is connected to blood, tools of surgery, and medicine. Especially surgery attracts these people. When their Destiny Number or Name Number or both get connected to the Birth Number, they are fit to become famous surgeons. Though even in any milder profession the "Martians" prove their skills, the vocations mentioned above will bring fame and fortune.

In this world of inter-dependence, the independent 9-people certainly would need help. It is provided readily by those born under Numbers 3,

5, 6, 8 and 9. Number 2 persons, though submissive to Number 9 in a few theatres of activity, will cause a lot of anxiety and worry to Number 9 persons. But with good Destiny and Name Numbers the 3, 5 and 6 people can be taken for sincere and long-lasting partnership

There are some peculiar traits with the Number 9 people. Their sense of freedom of independence makes them stubborn sometimes. It may cause some emotional upsets. But their tenacity helps them overcome any kind of obstacles in envisaging their plans. Thus, they become masters of their own destiny, - positively or otherwise!

NUMBERS AND NEWS

Can a body without head live....? Of course, only a **cockroach** can do!. It is said it can live without its head for **9 days** before it dies. A tenacious "Martian" it must be! (Among the humans a habitually ill-tempered man is called a **"headless"** man but he lives quite longer,-only to trouble others!)

CONCLUSION

There are lots of seminars, debates and disputes going on around us to discuss the subject of astrological sciences-both for and against! The so-called "pure" scientists vehemently oppose the learning or practice of the sciences like Astrology, Numerology etc., They simply forget that their forefathers in the field of science like Pythagoras, Hippocrates, Kepler and Newton and also contemporary scientists like Dr.C.V.Raman (Indian Nobel Laureate), Dr.Bryant Tuckerman, Dr.Robert O.Becker and many others did believe in the astrological subjects. Interestingly, many of them were even very good astrologers by themselves. None other than Dr.C.V.Raman said, "Fanaticism is the enemy of truth. Never become so scientific or religious that you forget to be human." But the tirade against the astrological sciences continues to this day!

Well, it is needless to say that as a traditional practitioner of Numerology, I am naturally drawn into the related discussion. The only question (after answering all the other questions) left to be **directly** answered is about the **infallibility** of astrological or numerological predictions, viz-a-viz the scientific theories.

Is science infallible? No doubt, science is based on the formulated knowledge of physical objects, their properties and their uses. The scientists experiment continually and finally launch a rocket. But it fails. Why should it? The most experienced surgeon with the most sophisticated equipments fails to save the life of his patient. What more, a few like him do very silly mistakes which, either kill or maim the patients! Why, the findings of a celebrated scientist like Dalton (who professed a theory that Atom was indivisible) later proved to be wrong! The belief that electrons are the only fastest particles on the earth has been routed in the recent years. If science is infallible and if scientists' conclusions cannot be disputed, why do we find so many failures, mishaps, accidents and deaths in the field of science? After all, astrologers and occultists deal with the human minds, whereas scientists deal with **the lives** of animals, plants and humans. Should they not be **more** infallible? These questions cannot be directly or plainly answered, because, both the groups have their own limitations! When a scientist believes only in what he sees, an astrologer believes in what he **sees, and feels (or senses).** Scientist proves his theories by the **effect,** whereas an occultist has to prove his theory by **cause** and **effect, the theory of cause being more complex than any science!**

The annals of occult history prove that the wise men of the world did believe in Numerology irrespective of their faith, race or country. They knew very well that the ancient Hindus, Arabs, Chaldeans and the Greek had explicitly and precisely revealed to the world thousands of years ago, what came to be known as scientific truths, **even without any known or recorded modern scientific instruments.**

Fakes and quacks are found in all fields of science. The field of occult sciences is not an exception to this rule. This malady can be averted if due recognition is given to the Astro-Numero Sciences and research is encouraged. **Calipha Mamoon-ur-Rashid,** a man of profound knowledge in sciences, ordered the translation of astrological works into Arabic in the 9th century A.D. and encouraged research. A befitting example to cite! The world has now turned a full circle and I am sure that Numerology will rule the roost in future. After all, who does not want to become lucky?

Voltaire, the eighteenth century French philosopher and an embodiment of enlightenment said: **"There is no such thing as chance; we have coined this word to express the known effect of every unknown cause!"**

Thank you, readers! Good luck to you and Good bye!

ADIEU!

Dear Readers,

You have finished browsing through this book, "My Fortune"! Now, you will naturally be tempted to know when and how you can find your fortune!

Having come to know how to use this book, you are ready to begin your quest for progress and prosperity with a greater degree of confidence. Well, you only need to remember, **"Numbers rule the world! "**

If you apply your knowledge derived from this book and become lucky in all your noble efforts, my mission of bringing out this treatise will be considered successful because, your fortune is "My Fortune"!

Wise men said, "It is so easy to be successful – if one can only get the right inspiration". May my humble efforts of giving you the right inspiration be fruitful!

With prayers in my heart for the success of my readers, I give rest to my pen – for the time being!

Good Luck!

V.S. Guruswamy

Here is the proof....!

"Strange theory, but there is a convincing coincidence of numbers in human life !"
His Holiness **POPE LEO XIII of VATICAN**
(The **257**th successor of St. Peter)

"The science of Numerology is the practical application of the fundamental laws of mathematics to the material existence of man!"
Sir.C.V. RAMAN
(Indian Scientist ; Nobel Laureate.)

"I am sorry I did not believe it first; the prediction by numbers is wonderful !"
His Majesty **MUZAFFAR - AL-DIN**
(Shah of Persia - **1900**)

"I do not believe in god or religion; but I am forced to believe in Numerology !"
Col. R.G. INGERSOLL
(Famous atheist and orator of U.S.A.)

Made in the USA
Lexington, KY
12 October 2014